What the Rich Don't Say about Getting Rich
Work Smarter
Live Better

(Text and Workbook)

from YourBodySoulandProsperity.com

Tom Marcoux
Executive Coach
Spoken Word Strategist
Speaker-Author of 35 books

A QuickBreakthrough Publishing Edition

Other Books by Tom Marcoux:

- Discover Your Enchanted Prosperity
- Emotion-Motion Life Hacks ... for More Success and Happiness
- Relax Your Way Networking
- Connect: High Trust Communication for Your Success
- Darkest Secrets of Persuasion and Seduction Masters
- Darkest Secrets of Charisma
- Darkest Secrets of Negotiation Masters
- Darkest Secrets of the Film and Television Industry Every Actor Should Know
- Darkest Secrets of Making a Pitch to the Film and Television Industry
- Darkest Secrets of Film Directing

Praise for *What the Rich Don't Say about Getting Rich* and Tom Marcoux:

• "Master Coach Tom Marcoux helps you make new breakthroughs to feel good, get more done, believe in yourself and enjoy each day. Create the success and prosperity you truly want!" – Dr. JoAnn Dahlkoetter, author, *Your Performing Edge* and Coach to CEOs and Olympic Gold Medalists

• "Tom Marcoux has distinguished himself as a coach, speaker and self-help author. His books combine his own philosophy and teachings, as well as those of other success experts, in a highly readable and relatable manner." – Danek S. Kaus, co-author of *Power Persuasion*

Praise for Tom Marcoux's Other Work:

• "Concerned about networking situations? Get *Relax Your Way Networking*. Success is built on high trust relationships. Master Coach Tom Marcoux reveals secrets to increase your influence."
– Greg S. Reid, Author, *Think and Grow Rich Series*

• "In Tom Marcoux's *Now You See Me*, the powerful and easy-to-use ideas can make a big difference in your business and your personal relationships." – Allen Klein, author of *You Can't Ruin My Day*

• "Marcoux's book *10 Seconds to Wealth* focuses on how each of us have divine gifts that we need to understand and use to be our best when the crucial '10 seconds' occur.... He identifies the divine gifts and shares how these gifts can help us create what we want in our lives, and the wealth we want." – Linda Finkle, author of *Finding The Fork In The Road: The Art of Maximizing the Potential of Business Partnerships*

• "In *Darkest Secrets of Persuasion and Seduction Masters: How to Protect Yourself and Turn the Power to Good*, learn useful countermeasures to protect you from being darkly manipulated."
– David Barron, co-author, *Power Persuasion*

• "In *Be Heard and Be Trusted*, Tom's advice on how to remain true to yourself and establish authentic rapport with clients is both insightful and reality based. He [shows how] to establish oneself as a credible expert."
- Arthur P. Ciaramicoli, Ed.D., Ph.D., author *The Curse of the Capable*

• "In *Reduce Clutter, Enlarge Your Life*, Marcoux will help you get rid of the physical and mental clutter occupying precious space in your life. You'll reclaim wasted energy, lower your stress, and find time for new opportunities." – Laura Stack, author of *Execution IS the Strategy*

Visit Tom's blog: www.BeHeardandBeTrusted.com

Tom Marcoux

CONTENTS*

* This table includes highlights. This book includes even more material!

DEDICATION AND ACKNOWLEDGEMENTS

This book is dedicated to the terrific book and film consultant, and author Johanna E. Mac Leod. It is also dedicated to the other team members.
Thanks to Barry Adamson II (of MyWordsForSale.com) for editing some sections. Thanks to Johanna E. MacLeod for your editing insights and for rendering the front cover and back cover.
Thanks for the guest authors and interviewees: Jeanna Gabellini, Randy Gage, Michael Hsieh, James Malinchak, Greg S. Reid, Ryan Peters, Morgana Rae, and Mark Sanborn. Thanks to my father, Al Marcoux, for his concern and efforts for me. Thanks to my mother, Sumiyo Marcoux, a kind, generous soul. Thank you to Higher Power. Thanks to our readers, audiences, clients, my graduate/college students and my team members of
Tom Marcoux Media, LLC.
The best to you.

Book One:

What the Rich Don't Say about Getting Rich

When has your life really been shaken?

I wrote this book because a close friend died. What killed him? A bad business model.

My friend's death shook me to the core.

In his sixties, he struggled every month to make the money for his rent until his last breath. His struggle also led to his body being a wreck.

I remember taking him to the hospital and staying with him for five hours. In his last month of life, we still talked about changing his approach to business. But he was not getting around to important tasks. He was not focused on making changes.

After he died, my grief hit me hard. Still, a phrase arose in my mind, "A bad business model can kill you."

I first thought of this book as an advanced course in wealth-creation, and I originally titled it *Get Real or Get Hurt—Get False Stuff Out of Your Way and Succeed!* However, some days later, another title arose just as I was settling to sleep. It wouldn't let me go so I wrote a lot of material quickly under the banner of *What the Rich Don't Say About*

Getting Rich.

We'll begin with something the Rich know: ***Jump when opportunity arrives. Have some inspiration, guard that momentum and take massive action.***

The universe likes speed. – Joe Vitale

Why? Often, timing is crucial. The radio was created on both sides of the Atlantic ocean at the same time. Multiple people get the same idea, and the Universe waits to see who goes into action fast.

As I noted, I took advantage of momentum and wrote lots of material for this book. Momentum is vital. Still, for our discussion about helping you become rich, momentum is *not* enough.

We need to add "Protect the Talent." That's something I learned while directing feature films. The smart director does two things: *"Guard Momentum and Protect the Talent."*

You, my friend, are the Talent (in filmmaking, the Talent are the actors and actresses). *We will **protect you** and your wealth-building efforts.*

This book is about **Sustainable Wealth.**

I'm not going to hold back. As an Executive Coach, I'm often called to help clients prepare to make powerful presentations. "Tell them the truth," I advise my clients who seek to make compelling speeches. I'm all about Authenticity. My emphasis is on what I call "A.E.E." — Authenticity, Evidence and Experience.

In my work with CEOs, I say: "I'm your Executive Coach. I'm *not* your employee. When we're in a session, I'm not your friend afraid to rock a friendship. I'm not a therapist. Some of my clients also work with a therapist. I'm in the business of *transformation*. I'm not in the business of Band-Aids. I'm here to support you to *see what you need to see* and do what you need to do to get what YOU want. That's my goal. That's my focus."

So here it is: *What the Rich Don't Say About Getting Rich.*

Why don't the Rich say these important details?

Here are some of the reasons:

- The don't want to appear weak
- They use strategy and keep secrets
- They do NOT know because they are like a natural athlete who does NOT analyze and communicate like a top coach
- The details do not fit the *myth* of the self-made millionaire
- They don't want to admit human failings and how they had to overcome some real internal blockages

We are going to do some myth-busting here.

Here's a first myth: Getting Rich is enough. Wrong!

Instead, I'll refer to a great phrase written by Julie Ann Cairns: *"Money easily flows into my life and my wealth continues to grow."*

Wealth is what we want. Wealth is a state of being. A number of people get rich and lose it all. They didn't train for it and they didn't set up a structured daily life and a support system to Keep Their Wealth.

But this is NOT for you.

This book is about telling the truth so you create Sustainable Wealth.

In many areas of this book, we're going to talk about three important elements: 1) Myth, 2) A Way You Can Get Hurt and 3) a Get Real Principle. This book includes:

Work Smarter:

1. Open Your Awareness

2. How You CAN Get Unstuck and Unleash New Opportunities for Yourself

3. Express Things Concisely

4. Get Real or Get Hurt – Get the False Stuff Out of Your Way – and Then Succeed

5. Your Springboard to Optimal Performance

6. Get in Motion

7. The One Question that Leads to Real Success

8. Challenge Your Habitual Thinking

9. Use "Both Ends Power"

10. Make Sure You Have Reserves

11. Focus on "What Reality Do I Need to Face?

12. Discover the Power of "Lead So I Follow, Speak So I Believe"

Drop What Does Not Work

1. When the Deep Lesson Raises You to a Higher Level

2. Don't Let Fear of Disappointment Limit Your Success

3. Don't Stick with Good; Step Up to Better

4. Don't Wait to "Fix Something Broke Inside"

5. Take Conscious Control of the Stories You Tell or They'll Strangle You

6. Drop the Life-killing "Idle Rich Plan"

These sections are designed so you can connect with the material and quickly answer related questions.

I use certain phrases so people understand them and remember the ideas. For example, as I coach CEOs, business owners and others, I express my phrase: *"Take Command, Focus Your Brand."* Even if you don't have a business, you have a personal brand (it is what you're best known for). Your clarity makes it possible to get more of what you want in life.

I'm not talking from theory. As a CEO, I lead teams in the United Kingdom, India and the United States of America. My strategies for success are proven to work where the rubber meets the road, and that requires you to take action as you learn from my story and the *experiences** of others in these pages.

As such, I encourage you to answer the provided questions as you read along.

(* When I talk with prosperous people, we talk about *experiences*. When they ask me about my favorite times, I mention fulfilling my childhood dream of walking on the ocean floor. I had the opportunity to do that at the Grand Cayman island. I liked that better than snorkeling in the Bahamas.)

When you answer the questions I provide in this book you gain a surprising advantage: You'll learn more about yourself and how to improve your daily actions and strategies in achieving success for your life.

Let's take the next step and focus on W.E.A.L.T.H.N.O.W.

W – Welcome and Release

E - Express credibility and connection

A – Adapt to losses and handle fear

L – Linger on the positive

T – Tell the story

H – Help people (communicate well)

N – Negotiate and "risk well"

O – Organize your Power Business Model

W – Wonder Your way to stronger

1. Welcome and Release

No rich person I know (including my friends) leads with "Oh, yeah, I've made big mistakes because of my own fear and anger."

The Rich learn to *Welcome the Lesson* and learn to *release* the tension and upsets along the way.

A lot is at stake.

I first talked about this in an article at my blog

YourBodySoulandProsperity.com:
What the Rich Don't Say about Getting Rich

"I'm afraid that if I really raise my income, some bad things will happen," my friend Sharon said. I listened with compassion and then shared some helpful ideas. When I speak on the topic "What the Rich Don't Say about Getting Rich," I share two blunt but useful details:

1) Accomplishments alone do NOT make you happy.

2) You better have self-care and a support system or things "blow up"!

1) Accomplishments alone do NOT make you happy.

What happens to a significant number of people when they attain financial freedom is that they get surprised about feeling bad, and elements of life fall apart. A number of authors including Jim Rohn and Peter H. Thomas reported that they hit millionaire status and then lost it all. (They persisted and gained the wealth again!)

Additionally, top author and business leader, Tony Robbins reports that when he had first earned a lot of wealth, things fell apart for him. He said, "I started to be harsh to people who didn't deserve it. I started to miss important meetings."

What is going on here?

I'll put this in one word **"connection."** That is, you need to focus on connection. If you want to enjoy happiness, you need to take significant steps to nurture real, loving, supportive connections in your life.

And it's not just having people who support you. **It's about you being committed to support others.**

Tony Robbins reports that he really did better in his business when he connected how many people he wanted to feed during Thanksgiving to how much he needed to expand his business. He said, "To feed all the people I wanted to feed, I needed to raise my business to the level of $3 million."

So if accomplishments, earning more and more money, taking more vacations, don't lead to happiness, what does?

I don't know what your destiny will be, but one thing I know: the only ones among you who will be really happy are those who will have sought and found how to serve. – Albert Schweitzer

Having purpose, meaning and some joy in the moment while being good to others comprise vital elements of a happy life.

I'll share something more about the process: I guide my clients to have more than accomplishment-goals. I invite them to have **"Green Tranquility Goals"** (or "Being Goals"). The idea is human beings need to support their own inner peace.

When you're prosperous, it's vital to stay connected to that part of you which is compassionate. When you're prosperous, it's easy to stay in a state of high expectations and when life has bumpy times to get into a state of frustration.

"… we're not actually in control, which is a pretty scary idea. But when you let things be as they are, you will be a much happier, more balanced, compassionate person." – Pema Chodron

This idea of "letting things be as they are" runs straight into the wall of "being a control freak." In my book, *The Hidden Power of the AND-Universe*, I note that we do better when we acknowledge how the universe functions. For example, you can:

- Focus on gratitude AND go for more (more prosperity, new and different experiences)
- Feel happy in the moment AND endure uncertainty

- Use strategy to make effective business moves AND do that which supports your spiritual well-being

"I equate ego with trying to figure everything out instead of going with the flow. That closes your heart and your mind to the person or situation that's right in front of you, and you miss so much." – Pema Chodron

The effective business person sees the signs of potential trouble ahead and they respond well to such signs. That means you keep your heart open and your mind free to be aware of the person or situation right in front of you.

For example, I'm quite selective in which clients I work with as an Executive Coach. I'm in the business of transformation and not in the business of Band-Aids. I begin a conversation with a prospective client with my mind open and aware. I approach the conversation with gentle curiosity, and then I can observe what is really present in the person and the situation.

So a useful Green Tranquility Goal is to condition your mind to shift to what's known as an Observer Mind. If you're feeling frantic, use the method of "Stop. Breathe. Observe." The idea is to disengage from an unhealthy pattern.

Now it's your turn. What can you do on a daily basis to support yourself in shifting from high intensity to inner calm?

2) You better have self-care and a support system or things "blow up"!

Robert Downey, Jr. rose to significant heights in the film industry, and then imploded.

He acted out, got into significant trouble and repeatedly went to jail. "You can't go from a $2,000-a-night suite at La

Mirage to a penitentiary and really understand it … [and] … I wouldn't wish that experience on anyone else, but it was very, very, very educational for me," Downey said.

Starting in July 2003, Downey began, he reports, a process that has kept him drug-free. He credits meditation, therapy, twelve-step recovery programs, yoga and the practice of Wing Chun kung fu to his recovery.

Downey also said that his wife significantly helped him overcome his drug and alcohol habits.

Let's pay special attention to the word **habits.** If you have the habit of not getting enough sleep, you could really self-sabotage your efforts to expand your prosperity. As an Executive Coach and Spoken Word Strategist, I support clients to create a transformation in their lives. Often this is the process of putting in systems and effective habits—and avoiding the faulty reliance on "willpower."

Why do things "blow up"? One detail is that when you're rich, you do not have to fit into structures that keep a lot of people grounded.

Recently, I gave a workshop on *Discover Your Enchanted Prosperity*, and I mentioned that a vital element is to notice how you're interacting with the world. Are you, in this moment, focused on love or fear? I suggest we add to "love" the words "be kind." Be kind to yourself. Treat yourself like you would a good friend. Be kind to others. Being kind and trustworthy are vital to getting more business.

"Man with unsmiling face should not open a shop." – Chinese Proverb

The idea is to take care of yourself so you have a smile. I've guided graduate students and my clients to develop the personal brand of 'T.H.O.R.' That is: Trustworthy, Helpful, Organized and Respectful."

Now it's your turn. How are you going to nurture your

own inner peace? Will you do kind things for yourself including enough sleep, good nutrition, exercise, and quiet time? How are you going to stay connected with other people? How will you shift your thoughts into a compassionate state of being?

Remember:

1) Accomplishments alone do NOT make you happy.

2) You better have self-care and a support system or things "blow up"!

* * * * * *

Our topic *What the Rich Don't Say About Getting Rich* lends itself to a vital realization: Those who stay rich learn to live life more often in the state of "love" instead of "fear." That is, *the Rich who are happy* learn to shift away from fear.

Recently, I was called to give a speech about how we can *make the shift away from fear* to love. **Here's the text of that speech:**

"I'm terrified. It's nighttime. Telegraph Hill, San Francisco. And this guy came close to killing me.

How did I get in this mess?

I have a question for you. How much of your day do you spend in fear? How much of your day is about doing things to stop bad things from happening? This is a spiritual idea— a philosophical idea. It's possible *not* to live in fear.

Speaking about preventing bad things from happening. Many of us in this room are still working on our taxes paperwork. I don't know anyone who says, "I *love* April 15th because I love giving my money to the government." [Audience laughed.]

So we take care of things. Still, we can shift how much time you spend in fear or love. Some people hesitate about the word *love*. I say, "Add to it 'be kind.'" Be kind to yourself. Be kind to others. This is a great place to be. Not in fear.

Now, what got me into the mess? Fear and anger. It's about 15 years ago. I'm there with my sweetheart. We're at Telegraph Hill. We're one block up the hill from her itty-bitty Toyota Tacoma truck. This HUGE Ford F-150 truck slams into that itty-bitty truck, smashing the tailgate. I'm seeing this—she's seeing this—from one block away. The big truck goes back and smashes the Toyota truck again!

Suddenly, I'm full of fear and I'm running toward that situation. The fear that I'm feeling is based on—it's *not* my sweetheart's truck. It is really her parents' truck. She's going to have all kinds of upset and bad feelings and dealing with the parents. I know if that truck driver succeeds in doing the hit-and-run thing, we got trouble coming.

So in fear for my sweetheart—it's my sweetheart—you don't mess with my sweetheart! [Audience laughed.]

I'm running down the street—straight toward the situation. My sweetheart—wise and rational—she's walking on the sidewalk. [Audience laughed.]

This guy takes his F-150 truck—have you seen one of those things? It's like a tank. It's huge as opposed to her *itty-bitty truck* [Tom's *little* voice—the audience laughed.]

He turns that big truck into me and hits me in the chest. [audience members gasp.]

He keeps pushing me with the truck after that. I end up holding onto the hood of the truck because where else will I go? He's already proven that he will kill me or at least hurt me because he's done it! He's hit me with the truck.

I am holding onto the hood. I am not that far from his face. There's the windshield right there. He's an older guy, a crazy guy, perhaps, an evil guy. I'm holding on and I'm yelling. Okay, I admit it: I'm screaming for help. Telegraph Hill, after 9 pm, San Francisco.

It's no movie. I don't have the arm muscles of Captain America. I can't go "Hello! I'm off the truck! You can't hurt me."

No I can't do that because I'm just a person hanging on. Until eventually, he stops. He's saying, while I was on the hood, "I've got an attack dog! I've got an attack dog, right here!"

And he opens the door, and the dog comes out. He says, "He's an attack dog!" And the dog looks back at him— "Attack dog—where?" [Audience laughed.]

So two things were great on that night. I didn't die. And second, it wasn't an attack dog.

What got me into trouble was fear and anger.

Would I do this again? No! I would take a cue from a wise and rational person—my sweetheart: I would walk on the sidewalk. [Audience chuckled.]

Because really it's money, it's trouble, maybe it takes a couple of years for the parents to mellow out about it. But if I'm not on the planet, I can't replace the money.

We're talking about: Get beyond fear. Get beyond anger.

In the moment, the idea is to **Stop. Breathe. And Observe.**

Get yourself out of the Ego-mind—it's made of fear.

Get into the Observer-mind—which is a place you can Stop, Breathe, Observe—and respond and not react.

I learned something fantastic from another woman Rekha (a group member). Three words: "Welcome and Release."

Welcome the lesson. I learned the lesson: Don't run down the middle of the street when Crazy Man is driving a truck. [Audience laughed.]

And Release. Release resentment, release anger. And it takes a process, but you begin with Stop. Breathe.

Let's all take a breath now. [Audience took in a slow breath.]

And let it out.

You do that three times, and it will take you to a different place.

You can get beyond the fear.

Stop. Breathe. And Observe.

And there's another thing I observed, and I take my cue from two wise women.

This is what I've observed:

Smart men listen to smart women next to them."

My above speech emphasizes "Welcome and Release."

Consider the importance of *Welcome the Lesson and Release Debilitating Thoughts and Feelings.*

Several times, I've heard people say, "That's won't work" or "Hey, your third book didn't sell, why don't you do something else. You'd be good as a manager..."

That's a whole different mindset. That the mindset of someone who focuses on earning an hourly wage. That's NOT an entrepreneurial mindset.

The Rich have the mindset of *what can I learn here? — and I'm moving forward with the next deal.*

How do you do Welcome and Release? This is really about how you condition your mind.

Research shows that people tend to have 10,000 to 70,000 thoughts a day, and the vast majority of the thoughts are simply repeated over and over again.

We, who build Sustainable Wealth, fill our thinking with thoughts better than fear — and we think such positive thoughts more often.

In my speeches, I often use a glass of water. I contaminate the water with a couple of ink drops. Soon the water transforms to a dark hue. Then I use a pitcher of clear, fresh water. I keep pouring until the inky water has vacated the glass. Now the glass is clear!

The metaphor is that you need to keep pouring clear, good ideas into your mind.

What kind of thoughts? Not fearful ones. Instead fill your mind with thoughts of love and kindness—toward you, your family, friends, clients and others.

The Power of Your Empowered Second Thought

You condition your mind to think an *Empowered Second Thought.* Here are examples:

- I'm afraid I can't make the payroll. **("Replace worry with action" ... "What can I do now that would help? I can list five people to call to ask for new business.")**
- That guy was rude! **("Does thinking about him strengthen me? No. I'll concentrate on healthy people who are a joy talk to.")**

The idea here is to choose to fill your mind with that which builds you up.

Myth: It's enough to just try to pick up the lesson.

A Way You Can Get Hurt: You could pick up the wrong lesson of "just try to be safe" or "avoid pain at all costs." Then you could be stuck and miss out on real opportunities.

Get Real Principle: Learn to "Welcome and Release." Learn to shift your focus. Use an *Empowered Second Thought.*

How will you practice "Welcome and Release"? Will you have a thorough conversation with a coach or therapist? Will you look for ways to release tough feelings of resentment and fear? Will you push through and avoid letting yourself be limited in your next actions?

The W.E.A.L.T.H.N.O.W. Strategy
Part 2

Express Credibility and Connection

The Rich know that you need credibility to close a sale. But there's more going on here. For example, to support credibility, you might include a professional biography on a flyer. Such a biography would highlight your accomplishments.

I have taught college level courses in Designing Careers, and during this time I guided students to write effective professional biographies.

My own professional biography is included in my flyers. At a recent *Discover Your Enchanted Prosperity* event, one of my team members placed a flyer on the seats for the attendees.

At one point during the event, I referred the audience to the flyer, and I said, "That paragraph about me that you see on the flyer shows my credibility. But that's *not* enough. What you need is BOTH **Credibility AND Connection.**"

The paragraph on the flyer read:

"Tom Marcoux helps you make Big Dreams come true. Known as an effective Executive Coach and Spoken Word Strategist, Tom has authored 35 BOOKS, with sales in 15 countries. Guest lecturer at STANFORD UNIVERSITY and feature film director, Tom knows how to TELL STORIES and make Your Brand Stand Out. He won a special award at the EMMYS and he directed a feature film that went to CANNES FILM MARKET. As a CEO, Tom leads teams in the United Kingdom, India and the USA. Tom guides clients and audiences (IBM, Sun MicroSystems, etc.) in leadership, team-building, power time management and branding. *The San Francisco Examiner* designated Tom as "The Personal Branding Instructor." See Tom's Popular BLOGS:

www.BeHeardandBeTrusted.com

www.YourBodySoulandProsperity.com

See Tom's Life-changing Video: "How to Believe in Yourself When Others Don't" (at YouTube.com—type in "Tom Marcoux believe") Tom Marcoux's Slogan: "Take Command, Focus Your Brand."

I continued, "There are people who are brilliant but they don't care about you. There are experts who are smart, but they don't listen to you and find out what you *really* need."

Here's something better: In what I do, you need to see me looking into the eyes of the audience members. You need to hear me listen carefully to questions coming from people's hearts. You need to hear me reply and share the truth and not just give you some 'slogan.'"

With the above comments, I was talking about *connection*. Credibility alone does not create wealth. People need to trust you. *Credibility AND connection are what attract great opportunities.*

Connection Often Comes from Being Vulnerable

Recently, I responded to a question on Facebook.com:

"Well said, Susan. Before I talk about something (like directing my first feature film), I talk about *where I came from:* I was a shy boy, terrified while playing a piano for seniors in a retirement home. My right leg fluttered as fast as a hummingbird's wings. I've learned that an audience will not come with me into new territory, if they don't know that I've been afraid and shy ... and that I had to train with mentors to do new things. Courage was necessary."

Audiences cannot relate to people who "seem to be perfect." They want to know you are a real person—someone who cares, who feels and who can understand their pain AND hopes.

Myth: Showing your accomplishments and credibility ensures trust.

A Way You Can Get Hurt: You'll miss out and opportunities that only arise when people can relate to you—person to person.

Get Real Principle: Learn to tell your story in a way that makes it easy for people to see you as a genuine and caring human being.

Do you talk to people in a way that sounds like you're reciting your resume? How can you make sure to listen to the other person more? How can you gently slip in a detail about what you learned? (People can relate to a person who says, "I learned that..." more than someone who pontificates and says, "Here's what you should do....")

_____

_____

_____

_____

_____

_____

The W.E.A.L.T.H.N.O.W. Strategy
Part 3

Adapt to Losses and Handle Fear

No wealthy person I've talked with started a conversation with "Oh, yeah. I've lost friends." Why not? Many rich people are quite alert to the impression they're making.

Perhaps, some fear an unspoken impression of "What? You've lost friends. What kind of monster are you?"

"If you want to be rich, you cannot be normal." – Noah St. John

The truth is: As you have more successes, some people will become more uncomfortable around you. It's as if your mere existence challenges less proactive people to assess their own lives. They may find themselves to be lacking initiative. That feels bad. And they don't like you for making them feel that way, so they want to get away or disparage what you do. Some people just do not want to reflect on how much more they can do in their own lives. Some people don't want the reminder.

You must listen to your own heart. For example, in college, I had a double-major. On a number of Friday nights, I walked into the college TV studio at 7 pm and then walked out of the TV studio at 7 AM the next morning. I would film segments of programs and edit videos. Why? That's when the equipment was idle. I could make extra high quality projects that would earn awards.

Still, I had a social life during college. I had two girlfriends in a row and then a third one for 2 ½ years until the end of college.

My point here is: The plan of 7 pm until 7 am was not "normal." At the college I attended, Friday night was party night.

My diligent work led to my winning some awards for my film/video work while I was in college. Those awards convinced people to join me as investors and team members for the first feature film I co-produced and directed. That jumpstarted my film industry career.

The Rich (who build business) work long hours. Why? They want to manifest something in the world!

As I wrote my books, I had two particular friends say disparaging remarks. They tried to talk me out of writing so much. Those two particular friends drifted away. What a relief! I felt so much lighter and more energized with them gone. As the phrase goes: Some people brighten a room when they leave it!

Handle Fear

What do we fear? Losses!

You cannot duck all losses. Life hands them out to the just and the unjust. The Rich know that they will do better if that take appropriate risks. More than that ... **The Rich learn**

from things as quickly as possible and then move on.

Several years ago, I wrote about the **Solution-for-Error Plan** in my book *Be Heard and Be Trusted*.

Now I want to revisit the Plan because it has a significant relevance to your creating Sustainable Wealth in that you'll save time, and your next efforts will be more productive.

Solution-for Error Plan

What if you had no fear of making mistakes? Would you try more things? Would your career take a leap forward?

Great communicators are effective because they take action, learn, and improve through feedback. If you do nothing, you cannot improve.

My clients use the *Solution-for-Error Plan* to gain these terrific benefits:

- Live an extraordinary life
- Remove self-defeating patterns
- Eliminate guilt feelings

You can live an extraordinary life

Top achievers who experience deep satisfaction and fulfillment have effectively learned how to stretch themselves, make mistakes, and learn so they can improve their performance.

The secret is that when we make a mistake, we quickly learn from it and do better. This is the reason I have developed the Solution-for-Error process.

An error doesn't become a mistake until you refuse to correct it.
– Orlando A. Battista

I have missed more than 9,000 shots in my career. I have lost almost 300 games. On 26 occasions I have been entrusted to take

the game winning shot, and I missed. And I have failed over and over and over again in my life. And that is precisely why I succeed.
– Michael Jordan

Anyone who doesn't make mistakes isn't trying hard enough.
– Wess Roberts

The people who take leaps forward in their lives engage in calculated risks. An old phrase says, "The person who never makes a mistake always takes orders from one who does." I have seen the value of this idea from talking with highly effective people. Entrepreneurs, and company presidents take calculated risks. They have employees who keep their heads down and seek only security. These employees prefer to accomplish routine tasks.

Creativity is allowing yourself to make mistakes.
Art is knowing which ones to keep. – Scott Adams

Researchers note that society provides big rewards to people who express their creativity and natural brilliance. Producers, actors, presidents, CEOs, and entrepreneurs are rewarded with astronomical salaries, bonuses, and residual income.

The idea is to harvest wisdom from your experiences. Think of the old phrase, "Good judgment comes from experience. Experience often comes from bad judgment." Let's harvest wisdom from our own experiences.

The Solution-for-Error Plan helps us to impact our subconscious minds quickly and powerfully with the lessons we need to learn so that we experience deep understanding. In this way, we empower ourselves.

When I did [the feature film] 1941, I felt I was made of Teflon. I felt that anything I put on film was going to succeed. I felt invincible. And in a sense, at that point in my life, the best thing that could have happened was the drubbing that 1941 got both from the critics and the public... I sobered up so quickly. [On 1941] I had gotten so precious... I should have had a second unit film the Ferris wheel [miniature special effects ... I was taking 20 takes on simple insert shots]. I couldn't let go. I couldn't share the workload with anyone. And I learned the greatest lessons of my career just from the experience of 1941... I went from the disaster of 1941 to my first day of shooting on Raiders [of the Lost Ark]. *In a sense, Raiders rescued me from getting self-involved with 'Oh dear, the movie is going to be a failure and all the critics will hate it'... By the time I did* Raiders, *I was humbled. Every shot was storyboarded. I was 14 days under schedule...* Raiders of the Lost Ark *was probably the most prepared I have ever been in my career to direct a movie, and it paid off. – Steven Spielberg*

I noticed that my clients felt limitations because of certain ideas they had read in books. Those books included good ideas, but the ideas were not integrated and hands-on. Many books do not give us a way to play with the material and feel it. Again and again, I've noticed people communicating lovely ideas that were merely rationally-oriented. To make massive progress, you need to feel it. As James Brown sang many years ago, "I feel good!"

With this insight, I developed the *Solution-for-Error Plan* to overcome the limitations that can arise in people from their mere reading of ideas in books.

Remove self-defeating patterns

Would your life leap forward to more enjoyment and greater success if you could break your self-defeating patterns? The Solution-for-Error Plan helps us pay attention to what went wrong and how to fix it.

For novice salespeople, self-defeating behaviors include devoting too little time to study and rehearsal, and then winging it. Winging it often leads to missed sales. Top producers study, rehearse their presentations and close more sales. With the Solution-for-Error Plan, we identify beneficial behaviors that can lead to breakthroughs.

Eliminate guilt feelings

How much lighter would you feel if you could eliminate guilt feelings?

The Solution-for-Error Plan helps us quickly develop a game plan for doing better. It is a planning process that allows us to escape from the endless loop of vague guilt feelings. Through this process, we can identify ineffective behaviors and focus on correcting them. We can say, "Okay, I blew it that time, but now I know how I can do better next time."

Psychologists have pointed out that punishment can often be ineffective because it only stops a behavior without providing productive alternative behaviors. The Solution-for-Error Plan helps us identify the solutions, or productive alternative behaviors, so that we feel relieved and empowered.

You always pass failure on the way to success.
– Mickey Rooney

Nobody has a problem; it's only a decision waiting to be made. If my so-called "problem" is the result of a bad decision that I made yesterday, then all I have to do is make another decision—a better decision—today! – Robert H. Schuller

As a general rule the most successful man in life is the man who has the best information. – Benjamin Disraeli

Some of the best information only becomes available when you take action and discover how you function in new and challenging situations. You learn where your natural brilliance is and which areas you need to improve. You may also learn that it is better to delegate certain tasks to people who have a natural talent in an area in which you do not excel.

A discovery is said to be an accident meeting a prepared mind. – Albert von Szent Gyorgyi

Many of the most successful people have noted that we learn more from a mistake or failure than from a successful outcome. The Solution-for-Error Plan helps you squeeze any experience and get the learning from it. You learn from what went wrong so you can correct it.

Failure is success if we learn from it. – Malcolm Forbes

Soon, I will show you the form that my company uses. We dare to achieve; occasionally, therefore, a situation turns out in a disappointing manner. The point is to learn, plan a better approach for future action and move on.

You miss 100% of the shots you don't take.
– Wayne Gretzky

It's better to explore life and make mistakes than to play it safe. Mistakes are part of the dues one pays for a full life.
– Sophia Loren

What if a 10-minute method could help you squeeze an experience or tough situation and learn what you need to learn from it? That method is the Solution-for-Error Plan.

Let's go into action and learn the Solution-for-Error Plan from this fictional example.

Solution-for-Error Plan (example)

Step 1: What's the error and what led to it?

Started a business with another person, with whom I did not develop a full written agreement. We were friends. We trusted each other as friends and thought that we were compatible as business partners.

What were the painful consequences, or the feelings you want to avoid?

It broke my heart when I found that I could not rely on my business partner to carry the ball when I was tired. I felt abandoned. Finally, the business was failing because it needed both of us to have full dedication in the startup phase.

Step 2 How can you avoid the error? What can you do better?

I can (a) study what I need in a business partner, (b) hold a number of meetings with any potential partner, (c) hire a well-respected consultant to help assess whether we are compatible as business partners, d) do a pilot program with the potential partner, and (e) write a full agreement, including an exit strategy.

Step 3 How can you compensate for your own tendency?

My tendency is to jump right in and not take time to look

at all potential problems. I can compensate for that tendency by hiring someone (who is highly recommended) to walk through the potential consequences with me.

Step 4   What did you do right?

I took action. I learned what does *not* work for me. Now that I know what my tendencies can create, I can be careful in similar situations.

Step 5   What does the solution look like? What does it feel like?

I gain the right business partner, whom I can trust. My ideal is the partnership of Walt Disney and his brother, Roy O. Disney.

Step 6   What are the benefits of the solution to you? To the team?

I will save myself from heartache and stress. With the right business partner, my quality of life will improve. I won't have to stay at the office all the time. I'll have time for my family. My team will feel better and be more productive when I am not stressed out.

Step 7   How can you reward yourself for taking action?

I will make relaxation appointments for myself: time for reading, taking hot baths, and walking in nature.

* * *

Now let us investigate the Solution-for-Error Plan in greater detail.

What's the Error and What Led to It?

I chose the word *error* with care. As we noted earlier,

An error doesn't become a mistake until you refuse to correct it.
– Orlando A. Battista

The first step is to face up to the error. We must acknowledge that we had something to do with the situation. We need to pay close attention to the details of what happened and then write down the error. Write what caused you to feel bad or what action you failed to take. For example, a workshop participant wrote, "I allowed myself to get tired, so that I was irritable later." Many people respect the one who admits an error and says, "With what I know now, here is my new plan … "

What led to the error?

Note the steps that led to the error. They may be something like staying up too late, or procrastinating on doing research to prepare for a first meeting with a potential client.

What were the painful consequences or feelings I want to avoid?

Identify the feelings related to the error that you want to avoid. For example, "I want to avoid feeling angry"; "I want to avoid feeling wronged"; or "I want to avoid feeling ignored." You can begin the process of dropping these feelings when you write them down in your Solution-for-Error Plan.

To create behavior change, we often need to stop and become aware of the price we have paid for the error. We need to recognize the error's consequences. The consequence of an error can be, "I feel that I failed the job interview because I didn't prepare beforehand by studying the company."

The good news is that as soon as you identify the error and what led to it, you have power that you didn't have moments before. You can take action from this moment onward to do better in life.

Now you're ready for the next question.

How Can You Avoid the Error? What Can You do Better?

Fear is the father of courage and the mother of safety.
– Henry H. Tweedy

Errors frequently occur because we didn't do something or we didn't prepare for a situation. We need to take preventative, proactive steps, which are like preventative medicine. This is proactive: you need to go out there and do it first, to prevent negative consequences from happening.

Consider every mistake you do make as an asset.
– Paul J. Meyer

Many of us remember procrastinating on a school paper until the night before it was due. Then we berated ourselves, telling ourselves, "I'll never let it get this bad again." Does this sound familiar? Does it remind you of how you prepare the paperwork for your taxes?

With the Solution-for-Error Plan, you'll have a powerful incentive to avoid letting this happen again, because you're going to remember how much pain the error caused. Also, you'll remember all the good things you can create in your life by taking proactive steps. You will have leverage on yourself in both directions: pain and joy (or pleasure).

An important component of this step is to note due dates for your proactive steps.

What can we do better?

In order to do better, we often need a team. In a team of people, one person can compensate for another's shortcoming.

Sometimes it helps to have a post-game review. For example, one friend told me about an error he experienced during a memorial service. A group of people gathered on a 70-foot yacht for the spreading of ashes in the ocean. Later, my friend told me, "I wasn't thinking straight. The grief had distracted me. If I was thinking clearly, I would have asked my wife to wear a life-jacket. No one wore life-jackets. Fortunately, no one fell over the side, even though the ocean was rough."

My friend was concerned about his oversight. He told me, "I am repeating this story to you so I learn the lesson."

Learning the lesson is the purpose of answering the question, "How can you avoid the error? What can we do better?"

How Can You Compensate for Your Own Tendency?

Harvest wisdom from an error and you are twice blessed: you won't repeat the error and you know what to compensate for.
– Tom Marcoux

Know your tendencies and compensate for them. People who accomplish more and feel inner peace have a different perspective on the mistakes they make. They understand that life is constantly offering us lessons. If we don't learn the lessons, the opportunities for learning (what we call our "problems") are repeated until we learn to take effective action. So we do well when we learn to compensate for a troublesome personal tendency.

To compensate is to make a correction. A salesperson may talk too much, leave out a detail, forget to ask for the sale, or miss the chance to engage a new person in conversation (and miss the resulting referrals). This salesperson can compensate by turning each mistake around. If he or she talks too much, the *turn around* is to listen more.

In your personal journal, write down some of your mistakes and find the *turn around* for each mistake. You'll make surprising progress when you follow through with this process.

What Did You Do Right?

A balanced view of our actions often reveals that we did something right. This section reminds us that certain behavior patterns *are still* valuable.

Sometimes we take the right action and something still doesn't work. Perhaps the interviewer was feeling ill, so the meeting went poorly in spite of our preparation. We don't always know. In any case, we need to keep up our morale by acknowledging our correct efforts.

Buckminster Fuller, who was considered a genius, emphasized the value of learning from mistakes:

If I ran a school, I'd give the average grade to the ones who gave me all the right answers, for being good parrots. I'd give the top grades to those who made a lot of mistakes and told me about them, and then told me what they learned from them.
– Buckminster Fuller

Constant effort and frequent mistakes are the stepping stones of genius. – Elbert Hubbard

[For my first album, Virgin Records] gave me no budget—practically no budget. I said "Prince, I will choreograph for you for free; you write me a song"... I worked with Kool and the Gang—[and I said] I need rhythm tracks; for your next tour [I'll choreograph for you]. I would go on and on, and I would barter deals. – Paula Abdul

Paula Abdul's first album was a big success, due in large part to the quality she gained with her bartered deals. But during her successful career as a popular music icon, she was not immune to feelings of self-doubt.

[I had] the real scary feeling of "Oh, no, I'm a fraud. I'm just waiting for them to find out. Fraud, fraud, fraud, fraud." Because I never knew that everyone else does the same thing. You end up becoming who you are by actually jumping into that circle of fear and doing it. And that's how you end up believing in yourself.
– Paula Abdul

We learn from Paula that the process is about doing and learning as you go.

We do not wait for the absence of fear. We use fear to help us learn what we need to do better.

This reminds me of how persistent Randy Pausch was in pursuing his childhood goal of becoming an Imagineer. He pushed beyond the first rejection letters that came to him from Walt Disney Imagineering. He continued in his efforts and eventually worked with Walt Disney Imagineering on Disney's *Aladdin*. Randy said:

The brick walls are there for a reason: they are there to give us a

chance to show how badly we want something. Because the brick walls are there to stop those people who don't want it badly enough.... If you lead your life the right way, the karma will take care of itself, the dreams will come to you.
— Dr. Randy Pausch

When we focus on what we did right, we often discover that we can feel good about some of our efforts. With this encouragement, we have the energy to refine our approach for the next occasion.

What Does the Solution Look /Feel Like?

If we think happy thoughts we will be happy. If we think miserable thoughts, we will be miserable. — Dale Carnegie

Identify what you can do that will prevent a similar error from occurring in the future. Perhaps you can rehearse or write out your sales pitch. You might find that exercising or changing your diet will provide you with more energy. These are actions you can use to replace self-defeating actions.

What are you going to get after you change your behavior? Are you going to serve more people, make more money, win an award or earn a vacation in Hawaii? You can use the Solution-for-Error Plan for every area of your life. You can use it to enhance your personal and business relationships.

Ask yourself, "What do I want to feel?" One client wrote, "I want to feel connected. I want to feel on course with my purpose." Often we want to feel powerful, strong, healthy, and joyful. It is crucial to target the feelings you want that the Solution can provide. You can feel prosperous, successful, and good about yourself.

What are the Benefits of the Solution?

Possible benefits, to you, to the team:

- I feel closer to my loved one.
- I have great job interviews.
- I feel relaxed.
- I feel the tension drain from my shoulders.
- I feel at peace more often during the day.

Here's an example of a valuable benefit, noted in this e-mail message from a client:

Tom, I had another social success after applying some of the techniques I learned in your workshop and book. I am on the social committee here at work. We had our company Thanksgiving lunch and Potluck last Thursday. I was on the decorating committee, and as it turned out, ended up being the hostess as well. As people brought in the food, they started asking me where to put things, and—Well, I ended up directing things. There was one moment of panic. I had left for a few minutes, to wash my hands and as I came back I heard the roar of voices. The room had been filling up in my absence, and the voices seemed to reach a deafening volume (anxiety attack), but I took a deep breath, told myself this was an improvisation of a party-scene where I was the confident hostess, and walked in. I used your method of "Act as if." Someone came up to me to ask if there was anything that still needed to be done, and that helped me get started directing things once again. Thanks Tom, for helping me through another tricky situation.

My client acted as if she were a confident hostess. With more practice, she is likely to find that she eventually feels like a confident hostess.

You gain strength, courage, and confidence by every experience in which you really stop to look fear in the face. You must do the thing you think you cannot do. – Eleanor Roosevelt

When you focus on the real benefit, you feel the energy to take an appropriate risk. We need to remember to take action in the manner of a person who believes in himself or herself. When you start to trust yourself, other people follow along and trust you, too.

How Can You Reward Yourself for Taking Action?

What tangible reward will you immediately present to yourself for changing your own behavior? I call this a self-reward. For example, I sometimes associate the purchase of a book with the successful accomplishment of a specific action. During my seminars, audience members suggest self-rewards such as a warm bath, reading a book, and getting a neck massage.

A special form of reward

The power to transcend fear comes from our burning desire and intense interest in doing the actual work. The work itself needs to be intrinsically enjoyable and valuable to us.

If you think that the finished book is of greater value than what you learned from the writing process, you are mistaken.
– Terry Brooks

If you don't think there is magic in writing, you probably won't write anything magical. – Terry Brooks

Many people would like to have written a book. But the effective writers I know *like to write*. Find what you like doing.

Principle
Use the Solution-for-Error Plan to help you learn and move on.

Power Question
If you knew that you could not fail, what would you attempt? (If you learn from each experience, there is no failure.)

On the next page, find a blank copy of the Solution-for-Error Plan form for your repeated use.

Solution-for-Error Plan

Step 1. What's the error and what led to it? What are the painful consequences, or the feelings you want to avoid?

Step 2. How can you avoid the error? What can you do better?

Step 3. How can you compensate for your own tendency?

Step 4. What did you do right?

Step 5. What does the solution look like? What does it feel like?

Step 6. What are the benefits of the solution to you? To the team?

Step 7. How can you reward yourself for taking action?

Copyright Tom Marcoux   YourBodySoulandProsperity.com

Myth: If you're careful, you can avoid many losses.

A Way You Can Get Hurt: When you hide inside your comfort zone, opportunities for advancement and Sustainable Wealth will zoom past you.

Get Real Principle: Become skillful in learning from your mistakes. Use the *Solution-for-Error Plan.*

Pick some mistake you made. Quickly jot your notes here. Use this space to fill out your Plan:

Solution-for-Error Plan

Step 1. What's the error and what led to it? What are the painful consequences, or the feelings you want to avoid?

Step 2. How can you avoid the error? What can you do better?

Step 3. How can you compensate for your own tendency?

Step 4. What did you do right?

Step 5. What does the solution look like? What does it feel like?

Step 6. What are the benefits of the solution to you? To the team?

Step 7. How can you reward yourself for taking action?

* * * * * *

More About Handling Fear

The Rich know that no matter how much they try, they are still going to be hit with haters' comments. So be it.

Here's something the Rich Don't Say about Getting Rich: "It hurts me a lot to receive such criticism." The Rich who are healthy do something so they can be ready and strong for the inevitable criticism.

My point is: You develop courage. No longer do you hide and try to avoid disapproval. You expect it and know you're strong enough to handle it! That's the stance of a Champion.

You CAN respond proactively when a customer/reader offers criticism. For example, some authors even offer an extra something when someone expresses dissatisfaction. This is about customer service. We take a cue from Disney Theme Parks. The team members seek to be extra helpful to the Guests (that's their term for a customer).

One author I know wrote in response to a negative review on Amazon.com: "Thanks for your response ... Send me an email at xyxy@gmail.com and I'll send you an ebook copy of my new, third book. Be sure to include "Sam at Amazon" in the subject heading of your email message. Thanks."

Here are my two favorite quotes about having courage to shine your light:

"Our deepest fear is not that we are inadequate. Our deepest fear is that we are powerful beyond measure. It is our light, not our darkness that most frightens us. We ask ourselves, Who am I to be brilliant, gorgeous, talented, fabulous? Actually, who are you not to be? You are a child of God. Your playing small does not serve the world. There is nothing enlightened about shrinking so that other people won't feel insecure around you. We are all meant to

shine, as children do. We were born to make manifest the glory of God that is within us. It's not just in some of us; it's in everyone. And as we let our own light shine, we unconsciously give other people permission to do the same. As we are liberated from our own fear, our presence automatically liberates others." – Marianne Williamson

"30% of the people will love you. 30% will hate you. And 30% couldn't care less." – Gabrielle Reece

So remember: 60% of the people won't be with you, anyway. Be sure to find your own "tribe."

"A tribe is a group of people connected to one another, connected to a leader, and connected to an idea ... A group needs only two things to be a tribe: a shared interest and a way to communicate." – Seth Godin

"The secret of leadership is simple: Do what you believe in. Paint a picture of the future. Go there. People will follow." – Seth Godin

Consider rewarding yourself for having the courage to take action and put your work into the world. How will you look for your own "tribe."?

_____

_____

_____

The W.E.A.L.T.H.N.O.W. Strategy
Part 4

Linger on the Positive

Researchers note that it takes 10 seconds of focused attention to get something positive into your long term memory. Successful people I have interviewed keep Progress Logs so they know the numbers. They know what they've accomplished.

Here's something the Rich Don't Say about Getting Rich: "I would learn *any* technique so I could get more out of myself and improve my productivity."

One of my clients is a sports psychologist who coaches Olympic Gold Medalists. There is no Olympic athlete who skips the vital step of having a coach!

So now, I'll act as your coach. I *strongly* invite you to **use a** ***Daily Journal of Victories and Blessings.***

For only 1.5 minutes, just before you go to sleep, you "linger on the positive." That is, you write down the positive things of your day into your *Daily Journal of Victories and*

Blessings. A victory is something good you accomplished. A blessing is something positive that arrived in your life like a surprise phone call from a friend.

Keep you "To-do list" separate from this *Daily Journal of Victories and Blessings.*

Think of your *Daily Journal* as an oasis.

I truly needed this *Daily Journal* when I was in college. I would go to bed sad every night because my To-Do List never became shorter. I went to bed thinking of all I had NOT accomplished that particular day. At 11 pm at night, I'd write a sad letter to my then-girlfriend. Bad idea!

In recent years, I have used a *Daily Journal of Victories and Blessings* every day. I go to sleep happy.

Remember in just 1.5 minutes, you'll linger on the positive. In this way, you'll exceed the required 10 seconds of focused attention so positive details go into your long-term memory.

Myth: You can just drift through your days and you'll feel okay.

A Way You Can Get Hurt: You'll lose personal energy if you allow your brain to only store negative details.

Get Real Principle: You have your power of choice to build yourself up! Use a *Daily Journal of Victories and Blessings.*

Will you begin a new habit of recording positive details (for just 1.5 minutes) in your *Daily Journal of Victories and Blessings?* When will you get your *Daily Journal?* (Make sure that the journal is something you like to work with.)

The W.E.A.L.T.H.N.O.W. Strategy
Part 5

Tell the story

Here's something the Rich don't say: "I had an unfair advantage."

Does Donald Trump emphasize that he went to his daddy and asked for a $1 million loan—and with that, Donald Trump started his business?

How about Bill Gates? Does Bill Gates emphasize that he went to his father and said, "Hey, Dad, loan me $50,000 so I can buy this operating system and then slap the name Microsoft on it?"

Those two details above do NOT fit **the story** of the *"entrepreneur starting from scratch without advantages."*

Rich people know that "people buy on emotion then later justify on fact." Stories inspire an emotional response.

All people have been conditioned to respond to stories.

An important detail is: *Who are you telling the story to?*

For example, in one of my *Discover Your Enchanted*

Prosperity workshops, an attendee asked, "How do you advise I change my video for YouTube.com so that I can get people to buy my product?"

The truth was: Her product was complicated and what she really wanted was to get a Board of Advisors and partners to invest in her company and product.

I replied, "Your product and your situation is about attracting early adopters. We need to study the targeted early adopters for your specific product."

I continued, "I'm not an early adopter. You know the Titanic? I wouldn't have been there. I'm not going to be on the maiden voyage of anything!" [Audience members laughed.]

My point here is: You need to strategically build your story to engage your specific target market.

Part of the process is to get really clear about your own brand. Here is a formula is use with various clients:

Tom Marcoux's Branding Formula:
I help people   _____
to achieve   _____
They feel   _____
My clients say   _____

Here's another way to view this:
I help people __(verb)__
to achieve __(results)___
They feel __(successful, relieved, happy about, more effective)___

My clients say: Joe is so trustworthy and smart about marketing that my sales went up 37%. [an example]

Example:

I help people create High Trust Relationships
to achieve more success and even happiness.
They feel excited and even relieved.
My clients say: "Tom coached me to get more done in 10 days
than other coaches in 2 years."

Use an Empowering Question to Help Improve Your Personal Brand:

Your personal brand is your answer to the question: **"What am I best known for?"**

Your personal brand is also a promise of performance.

What can people count on you to accomplish that benefits them?

Now, here's an Empowering Question:

What do I do that's easy for me, hard for others and people want to pay for?

Story is crucial for you to engage customers. Still, who has to be sold on your enterprise first? YOU.

Get Smart About How You Tell the Story to Yourself

As an Executive Coach, I often have a client who gets wonderfully and pleasantly surprised. "You mean I CAN DO THAT? That would be great!" This delightful surprise often arrives on the heels of my leading the person through the following four questions:

4 Questions for Your Niche Brand:
1. Who do you want to help?
2. Where's the fun?
3. How are you similar to your target market?
4. How can you heal them and a part of you?

I was working with Sara who said that she wanted to help people step out of the darkness. I celebrated her intention. "I said, You CAN do that."

Then I asked, "Where's the fun?"

"Traveling and speaking," she replied.

"Where?"

She replied with, "Oh, maybe Colorado, Ohio."

I pressed her to where she'd *really* like to go.

Finally, the 4 Questions yielded:

She can teach women at a conference in Hawaii!

Myth: Giving the facts convinces people.

A Way You Can Get Hurt: You'll miss getting the *Golden Yes!* from people.

Get Real Principle: Refine your story. Rehearse it *a lot.* And move the person's heart. Get that *Yes!* you really want!

Write down the ideas for Three Possible Candidates for your Story that Moves Peoples' Hearts.

1

_____

2

_____

3

_____

The W.E.A.L.T.H.N.O.W. Strategy
Part 6

Help people (communicate well)

Communicate that you care. That's it! There's no excuse if you fail to let the other person know that you are paying close attention to their concerns.

I guide graduate students and clients to have a great personal brand. That's the answer to the question: *What are you best known for?*

My clients learn to communicate "T.H.O.R." They are Trustworthy, Helpful, Organized and Respectful. By the way, in my book *Relax Your Way Networking*, I share what I call "The 3 Magic Words of Networking"—**Help Them First.**

1. Avoid taking people and situations for granted

If you find yourself emotionally shut down, take this as a *"Red Alert Situation."* By this I mean, you need to recover the compassionate side of yourself. Without compassion, you're not fully human—and you risk missing out on genuine happiness. Right this moment, write down something that you better pay closer attention to. How can you demonstrate that you care and that you appreciate someone or some situation in your current life?

----

2. You must push yourself to stay compassionate.

In her book, *No One Understands You And What to Do About It*, author Heidi Grant Halvorson wrote: "The researchers found [that] ... powerful people will pay attention to you when doing so facilitates *their* goal." Halvorson continued, "There is a really important insight in this research. For the powerful, your *instrumentality* is key. Frankly, it is all that matters. What can you do to help powerful people reach *their* goals? ... If they invest time and mental energy into really 'getting' you, what is the potential return on their investment? ... Instrumentality isn't about being nice—it's about being useful."

Here's something the Rich Don't Say About Getting Rich: "I'm blinded by my obsession for my goals. And people know that I don't give a damn about them."

Several reasons arise for not saying this comment. They include the goals of not appearing weak and not appearing unaware. Further, the Rich do not want to appear stupid for ignoring something vital to success: *Creating and nurturing the important relationships that facilitate success.*

Here's the insight I'm bringing to you: **You must push yourself to stay compassionate.** Why? If you lose touch with your humanity, you'll "blow up." You'll treat other people harshly by reflex.

Further, if you lose your compassion, you'll even lose compassion for yourself. You'll create your own misery. Lots of money and no happiness—that's an awful plan.

How do you keep your compassion alive?

It's been proven that if you shift your focus, you CAN see things from another person's point of view. How? Use these words to activate the shift: **"How would I feel if I ____?"**

For example, some adults were having difficulty with their elderly parents who bitterly complained during every visit.

One woman said, "I thought about how would I feel if I was stuck in a bed 17 hours a day and felt pain most of the time." She reported that *her perspective shifted.*

Another way to keep your compassion alive is: Take good care of yourself. If you're in pain, if you're exhausted, you do *not* have the space to pay attention to another person nor his or her situation.

If you find that you're having trouble being compassionate towards others, connect with a part of yourself that needs healing. Perhaps, you can help younger people who are experiencing the pain that you once did in your earlier years of climbing the ladder of success.

You'll feel compassion for people who are similar to your younger self—when you were in pain. *Help them but don't deny them the experience of stretching.* For example, some parents will say, "You can earn half the money for that [top bicycle, top recording equipment, etc.] and then we'll come in and help with the other half."

We'll now cover another element of keeping your compassion alive: nonjudgment.

Nonjudgment

We should not pretend to understand the world only by the intellect. The judgment of the intellect is only part of the truth.

- Carl Jung

Adopting an excessively critical perspective is a habit that can deny you much enjoyment and fulfillment in life. It is like a door that slams shut automatically. As Carl's comment implies, many of us may believe that our intellect holds all the answers. This denies us the power of intuition. Also, a number of people feel that human beings can access Higher Power's guidance.

The most beautiful thing we can experience is the mysterious. It is the source of all true art and all science. He to whom this emotion is a stranger, who can no longer pause to wonder and stand rapt in awe, is as good as dead: his eyes are closed.

– Albert Einstein

We cannot get to the "mysterious," as Albert suggests, if we allow intellectualism to shut down our feelings, intuition, and empowering thoughts.

A Life Affirming Difference

I have repeatedly heard friends and audience members say things like, "Judgment is important. That's how I learn from the past, so I won't make the same mistakes again."

On the surface, this makes sense. And, yet, for those of us who want to experience more times of fulfillment, inner peace, and expanded success, there is an alternative.

To foster the optimal mindset, I recommend substituting the word *discernment* for *judgment*. To be a "discerning person" implies flexibility, acceptance, and calmness. To be a judgmental person implies rigidness, defensiveness, and superiority.

[The English language is a living entity. At the moment, a number of authors are writing about discernment and judgment, advocating for the adoption of a distinction between the two terms, along the lines advocated here.

To further support the idea of using the two words differently (discernment and judgment), consider commentary on how the word *judgment* can function ambiguously. Rick Porritt observes that two different Greek words were originally used in the *Bible,* but translated into English as one—judgment. He discusses an occasion in Luke where the Greek word contains the idea of "condemning" (which is therein frowned upon). On the other hand, on an occasion in Corinthians the Greek word means "scrutinizing" (which is therein approved of). *To Judge or Not to Judge?: Judgmentalism & Discernment,* Rick Porritt.]

Discernment is a softer process that still allows for recognizing that a past behavior did not give you what you wanted so you can choose to act differently in the future.

On the other hand, *judgment* as personified in judgmentalism includes the dominating acts of the courts, who use judgments as instruments of force to silence opposing viewpoints. Whatever value this has to litigation, this process can cause havoc in our spiritual lives.

So right now, consider adopting the process and attitudes of discernment.

Because, once one acts like a judge, pronouncing one truth, one becomes blind to alternative viewpoints. For example, I had two clients, Matt and Kaya, a couple in the throes of a devastating argument. As an impartial third party, I could see that they were both right in a way. But they had already rendered their judgments about one another. Their rigid judgmentalism threatened their relationship.

Instead, they could have discerned what was working or not. They could have recognized that they were both good people with different perceptions and priorities. That would have been a good foundation for resolving their differences.

Therefore, I invite you to adopt the flexible stance. Though it's easier to default to judgmentalism, discernment is more enriching, bringing us access to all the viable viewpoints. We avoid elevating ourselves to a superior position.

Your task is not to seek for love, but merely to seek and find all the barriers within yourself that you have built against it. - Rumi

Indeed, some of my friends have said that, during moments of arrogance, the universe took them down a peg or two. For example, one speaker I know was being abrupt with people because, she said, she was "so busy and in demand." Then one of her best clients suddenly dropped her services. She learned that bringing kindness to people is as important as bringing intellectual solutions.

Help Yourself

Be sure to take care of yourself. It is folly to try to build a house on a shaky foundation.

In spiritual circles, people hear, "You need to forgive." I offer another idea for those of us who view "forgive" as "let them get away with it." Try something else. Say (to yourself) "I *release* me. And I release you. I'm not the same as I was [yesterday]. And you're not the same. *I release me.*"

If you practice releasing, you may awaken your compassion.

Myth: Arrogant people can rise by shear will alone and they do not have to be good to anyone.

A Way You Can Get Hurt: Arrogant and disconnected people often get a circle of people hoping and even plotting for them to fail.

Get Real Principle: You must push yourself to stay compassionate.

What specific things can you do to help others?

The W.E.A.L.T.H.N.O.W. Strategy
Part 7

Negotiate and "Risk Well"

"You don't get what you deserve; you get what you negotiate," author and negotiation strategist Chester L. Karrass wrote.

To negotiate well you need courage and you need to be strong. **You need to be strong in the other parts of your life.**

If you're exhausted, you cannot negotiate well. So you log your sleep and make sure you get more sleep. Take power naps.

If you don't get exercise and your body is a wreck, you'll take the measly first offering from the person on the other side of the table.

If your relationship with your romantic partner is a wreck, you may be distracted and may fall apart during negotiations.

I wrote a whole book on negotiating titled: *Darkest Secrets of Negotiation: How to Protect Yourself, Overcome Intimidation,*

Get Stronger, and Turn the Power to Good.

One time a person looked through the book and said, "Hey, there's some self-help material in here." I replied, "It's not just about negotiating techniques. Other people can write a book on that. I write about how you can be strong and stand up for yourself!"

Here I want to introduce you to ideas first mentioned by author and master negotiator Herb Cohen: "L.A.R." and "M.S.P."

L.A.R. stands for Least Acceptable Result. If you were selling a used car and you felt that the Least Acceptable Result was $5,000, you would find anything over $5,000 to be "a win."

M.S.P. stands for Maximum Supportable Position. You are being sized up by the person on the other side of the table. If you ask for something astronomical, they might just conclude that you're crazy or at least a complete amateur, whom they want to avoid.

Do your research. Identify a good L.A.R. and a good M.S.P. Then you'll start from strength.

Myth: Negotiation is only about techniques.

A Way You Can Get Hurt: People will see through your techniques and find out that you're either uninformed or weak.

Get Real Principle: Do two things right. Build a good working relationship and develop yourself so you really are strong.

How to "Risk Well"

What is a good risk?

Consider these factors:

- Can I do this without "losing the store"?

- Will this give me experience so I can do better the next time?
- Will this show the world what I can do on a small scale? Will this line me up for bigger opportunities?

Film director Gareth Edwards made a tiny budget feature film, *Monsters,* and did the special effects on his home computer in his bedroom. After the film debuted, he was hired to direct *Godzilla* for a budget of $160 million. Imagine that pressure! Then he was offered *Rogue One: A Star Wars Story* to debut in 2016, the year following the debut of *Star Wars: The Force Awakens.*

My point is: **Take appropriate risks and show the world what you can do on a small scale.**

By the way, figure out how you can regroup if your project actually failed. Then *you know* you can face trouble and carry on.

"To stand out, find out what you stand for." – Tom Marcoux

As part of your journey in learning to "risk well", I invite you to consider having a *Milestone Binder.* You'll take action and try new activities—and then note your experiences in your Milestone Binder.

You note things that you try for the first time.

In my own Milestone Binder, I have these entries (that have taken place over the years):

The First Time . . .

1) directing a feature film
2) auditioning for a commercial
3) performing as lead singer of a band
4) addressing an audience of 703 people

5) teaching MBA students at Stanford University.

6) having a face-to-face meeting with a literary agent

7) helmet-diving.

To put it in few words, I've faced risk often and sometimes I've failed.

I've learned that you need to keep swinging the bat in order to have some home runs.

I've also learned three important strategies **(the 3 R's)** related to facing risk and disappointment.

Strategy #1: Reduce the downside

When I do a project, I make sure that the budget is NOT excessive and does not bring down the company. In fact, I have a couple of projects going at one time because I know some projects fail to bring in a preferred income. As a couple of millionaires have said, "You only have to be right 51% of the time."

Strategy #2: Rehearse

Before any first time event, rehearse. In fact, I encourage my clients and graduate students to use this practice: Any time you feel fear, rehearse.

Strategy #3: Regroup with a "Celebrate Someone Disagrees" Celebration

I remember when my second book came out. One of my close friends trashed it. In my mind, I had this thought: "Well, I didn't write it for *you*."

No matter what value you bring with a project, someone is not going to like it. Instead of letting that stop me, I realize that resistance and dislike for any project just happens.

So I invite you to have a "Celebrate Someone Disagrees"

Celebration.

For example, someone close to me had her book rejected by a committee at a top publishing company. I said, "I'm with you. It hurts. And tell me when you might want to celebrate."

"Celebrate?" she asked.

"Yes, celebrate your courage to put something out into the world. Celebrate your courage and persistence to get something done! And finally celebrate that if you don't put anything into the world then no one will disagree about the value of the project. I call it 'Celebrate Someone Disagrees.'"

My friend got into the swing of things and said, "Sushi! I want to celebrate with sushi!"

Great!

In summary, to feel those moments of triumph and feeling proud of yourself, you'll need to face risk and disappointment.

People who succeed face adversity. They keep going. One thing they avoid is the regret of not having taken action.

I do not regret the things I've done, but those I did not do.

– Rory Cochrane

Enjoy the best in life. Face risk and disappointment and *feel alive!*

Living at the top of your game involves taking appropriate risks. To do that, you need to be able to think clearly. Pay attention to what helps you calm down.

Some of my clients, just before they go to sleep, ask a question: *Why is it easy for me to fall asleep?*

Here's an example of one client's nightly paragraph she tell herself just before sleeping:

Why is it easy for me to fall asleep?

Because I'm safe. Because God has a plan for me.

Because I'll feel refreshed on waking up tomorrow.
I'll wake up thinking: "Thank you, God for this new day for love, prosperity and excellent health."

"Success is on the other side of your comfort zone."
– Orrin Woodward

The Rich know that taking appropriate risks brings on enjoyable rewards.

Myth: You can avoid failure by avoiding taking any risks.

A Way You Can Get Hurt: You'll stay stuck if you do not step out of your comfort zone.

Get Real Principle: Become strategic about risk.

Here's an idea: "You can't fail with an experiment." That is, you try something and see what you learn.

What things can you try to move forward in a positive direction?

_____

_____

_____

_____

_____

The W.E.A.L.T.H.N.O.W. Strategy
Part 8

Organize Your Power Business Model

At the beginning of this book and in another section, I mentioned that a close friend, Frank, died due to a Bad Business Model. That is, up to his last breath, he struggled to earn enough income for that month's rent payment.

What is a bad business model?

It's the opposite of **a Power Business Model which has these elements:**

- You get repeat business from customers.
- You can guide customers to order more and more from you.
- You do NOT have to "be at the store" all the time.
- You build assets so your business gains value and you can ultimately sell the business (if you want to).

If you do not develop a business that has the above

elements, then you've "bought yourself a job."

It's *not* a business if you only work within a situation of being paid by the hour. We know that a job for many people is "show up for X hours and get paid Y money."

When your business works well, it's making money while you sleep.

Fill in the following with your first ideas for
Your Power Business Model

How you get repeat business from customers:

_____

How you can guide customer to order more and more from you:

_____

How you can form alliances or get virtual contractors—so you do NOT have to "be at the store" all the time

_____

How you build assets so your business gains value and you can ultimately sell the business:

_____

Other ideas:

_____

For example, I work with my team in my company Tom Marcoux Media, LLC to expand what we offer with these franchises:

Jack AngelSword (fantasy-thriller)

Jenalee Storm (Young Adult fiction)
Crystal Pegasus (fantasy for children)
TimePulse (science fiction)

We'll now talk about focusing your efforts by using a One Page Business Plan.

One Page Business Plan

Would you like to get more done and feel better about your life? When you focus on what you really want and develop a focused-plan, you'll feel better because you'll have both marching orders and true clarity.

On the other hand, without a focus point, we scatter our energy. I've developed the *One Page Business Plan* that I carry with me every day.

The ultimate benefits of a One Page Business Plan are:
- more productivity
- time savings
- clarity
- focus on activities that generate personal good feelings and fulfillment
- focus on activities that generate profit

An old phrase is: "You get what you think about most." When you use a One Page Business Plan, you're thinking in a focused and positive manner.

Here are the topics that go on one 8.5 x 11 inch sheet of paper (suitable for a wallet or purse):

One Page Business Plan

- Mission:

- Top Goals with Due Dates:

- Ultimate Goals:

- Current Areas to Feel Good About and Feel Excited About (What works)

- Current Leadership-Growth Areas (includes keeping team members strong and happy)

- Current Areas to Measure

- Current Areas to Improve

- Current Areas to Watch Carefully (monitor and improve)

- [Your First Name,] What Are You Looking Forward to Experiencing and to Feeling?

- 3 Levels of Goals: Good, Excellent, Amazing!

- Effort Goals . . . Result Goals

- Other Notes:

© *Tom Marcoux   Tom's Blog: BeHeardandBeTrusted.com*

The *One Page Business Plan* is the center of *Focus-Point-Mastery*. The idea is to approach your daily life like you're a master of Power Time Management. It's really about you becoming skillful in making things happen that increase your joy and fulfillment.

Since there are 11 elements of the One Page Business Plan and I want to summarize the overall process, I'll now provide a few details per section.

1. Mission

It's best when your mission is beyond just making money. For example, my company's mission is: *We create energizing, encouraging edutainment for our good and humankind's rise.*

I include "our good" because strong and happy people make things turn out better for customers. Further, I make sure that team members fulfill some personal goals. It keeps them motivated to devote their best efforts.

2. Top Goals with Due Dates

Due dates are crucial; otherwise, things are too vague. Without due dates, productivity suffers.

3. Ultimate Goals

One of my ultimate goals is for my fantasy-thriller franchise *Jack AngelSword* to be so successful so that near the end of my lifespan Disney will want to buy my company. This would insure that millions of people would be served by my work beyond my lifetime. How fun!

4. Current Areas to Feel Good About and Feel Excited About (What works)

Never underestimate the power of good, empowering feelings to carry you forward through any tough times.

5. Current Leadership-Growth Areas (includes keeping team members strong and happy)

Every leader has weak areas and blind spots. It's good to identify details to work on. Good leaders develop loyal and productive teams.

6. Current Areas to Measure

I emphasize: *"Don't guess. Measure for success."* For example, I identified a target of writing 400 words a day which alerted me that I had 170 days to go on a certain project. A benefit of measuring your progress is that you raise your own morale!

7. Current Areas to Improve

People who are serious about increasing their joy and fulfillment monitor how they're currently doing. They also identify how they can get better at what they do.

8. Current Areas to Watch Carefully (monitor and improve)

In business, leaders are advised to pay attention to Key Performance Indicators and "critical measures." Two such measures can include number of sales meetings and closed sales. Which critical areas do you need to monitor and improve?

9. [Your First Name,] What Are You Looking Forward to Experiencing and to Feeling?

Imagine this: you can clearly see what all of your big efforts are going to bring to your life. Such clarity can motivate you on a daily basis. What do you really want? Research data shows that many people simply want to feel happy and secure. How will accomplishing your business goals bring you such feelings?

10. Three Levels of Goals: Good, Excellent, Amazing!

Some people set goals that are too extreme. Others set goals that are too low and un-motivating.

I've learned that it's better to set three levels for goals: Good, Excellent, Amazing!

Here's an example:

One author I know sells 25 books each month. She can set a "Excellent" goal of 300 books. Then, for "Amazing!" she can set 4,000 books sold per month. To reach for the 4,000 level, her thinking must expand. Now, she's thinking of ideas like: "How can I team up with other authors so that we can promote our respective books to each other's e-lists?"

Three levels of goals gives you the space to think bigger and allow the universe to give you "happy surprises."

11. Effort Goals . . . Result Goals

In sales, an Effort Goal can be "make 30 marketing calls this week." A related Result Goal might be "gain three new clients." We notice: You can't get a Result Goal without taking action on an Effort Goal.

You can be proud of yourself for your actions on Effort Goals regardless of whether you meet a Result Goal this week or next month. The truth is: Result Goals are often based on things out of our control. The good news is that we can control our personal efforts toward Effort Goals.

* * *

Here is the essence of the One Page Business Plan:
We are motivated by what we want to feel.

We generally change ourselves for one of two reasons: inspiration or desperation. – Jim Rohn

Another way to look at this is:
What do you want to feel?
And what do you want to STOP feeling?

Many people are wired in such a way that they'll do more to end some form of pain than make the efforts for something vaguely positive.

The One Page Business Plan helps you identify your clear, focused plan of action.

I've noticed that many people will put more effort into planning a vacation than planning their life.

But this is NOT for you.

Use a One Page Business Plan that's focused on business-related goals, and you're likely to expand your success. More success may lead to more vacations!

Principle
Using a One Page Business Plan helps you focus on critical factors to improve both your business efforts AND your feelings of fulfillment.

Power Question
What would you put into the categories of your One Page Business Plan?

* * *

A vital component of your business plan is to **Set Criteria**

for Excellence. When a complicated solution is needed, encourage yourself to note aspects of an ideal solution. You set criteria for what a good solution would look like.

The idea is to identify what creates excellent results. Often, we need to avoid getting bogged down in trying to make things perfect. Instead, we can focus on a project that creates excellent results.

For example, years ago, I considered making a short film titled *Dimension Man*. First, I set criteria for a project that was both feasible and worthwhile:

1. A film that was edgy
2. A film that was simple enough to produce quickly (because I was pre-booked with other projects)
3. A film that had both a startling first image and final image
4. A film that had characteristics that would make it a likely contest winner
5. A film with a modest budget

With the criteria set up, I could, as the leader, evaluate whether the project was a "go" or if it would be better to abandon it.

To create consensus, sometimes it's easier to have people toss in ideas about what a good solution will look like. Then, a meeting facilitator can say, "Well, it looks like this solution matches criteria 1, 2, and 3. How about if we move forward with this solution?"

Principle:
Encourage your team to *Set Criteria for Excellence* to improve results.

Power Question:
How can you help the team Set Criteria for Excellence?

Myth: It's okay to have vague notions about your business goals and how you can experience feelings of fulfillment.

A Way You Can Get Hurt: You might reach some business goals but feel vaguely unfulfilled. Such feelings may lead to self-sabotage.

Get Real Principle: Use the One Page Business Plan to stay connected to the truth of both your business goals and "personal strength" goals.

Write down your first ideas about your business goals that you can achieve AND actions that provide you with feelings of fulfillment.

_____

_____

_____

The W.E.A.L.T.H.N.O.W. Strategy
Part 9

Wonder your way to stronger

"If you want to be rich, you cannot be normal." – Noah St. John

When I say "wonder your way to stronger", I'm emphasizing that you need to question how you do things. *Are you doing things in a way that results in increasing your strength?*

Will something you do enhance your negotiating stance?—for example.

In one of my workshops, a savvy participant said, "I want to learn how to increase my leverage."

On the topic of leverage, I'll now share my experience of sending a book proposal to a top agent (some years ago). Within one hour of receiving my book proposal, he called me. Wow! Good news! Did he concentrate on the value of my book? No. He concentrated on the marketing plan.

Ultimately, he passed on the book. I realized what was

going on. This was *before* I had been a guest instructor at Stanford University and before I had thousands of contacts via Linkedin, Twitter, Facebook and more. Additionally, this was before I had written 35 books.

I was missing something. **Leverage.** Leverage includes having 1) special knowledge, 2) access to target markets and 3) influential contacts.

Here's something the Rich Don't Say about Getting Rich: It's not just about being good at what you do—it's about having leverage! One of my favorite questions to ask myself is: **"Does this strengthen me?" Look for ways to improve your position of leverage.**

Additionally, guard your personal energy. If an extended family member constantly berates me, I reduce the time in that person's presence. It comes down to my paying attention to my own answer to the question: "Does being around this guy strengthen me? Or does it tear me down?"

To create Sustainable Wealth, you must get stronger. In particular, *people are going to get angry at you*. The phrase "haters are going to hate" is true. There is a meme bouncing around Facebook: An image of Oprah Winfrey has the phrase: **"If you can't handle being talked about, you're not ready for success."**

Myth: You can be average. You do not need to be stronger than ever before.

A Way You Can Get Hurt: You won't be able to endure and persist. You may give up just a couple of feet before you succeed.

Get Real Principle: Continually assess the current situation. Ask yourself: "Does this strength me?"

Wonder how you can get stronger. What simple daily

practices will make you stronger? Do you need to start or improve upon your own exercise program? Do you need more sleep? Are you losing energy to negative people or even watching negative television programs?

_____

_____

_____

_____

_____

How You Can STAY RICH (Stay Strong)

I'm talking about Sustainable Wealth. In two words: **Stay Healthy.** Stay healthy in mind, body and soul. Stay healthy in how you bring in income and how you're generous. And how you save money. Keep structure in your life. This is the downfall of many new millionaires. They think that they can "do anything I want." *But dropping structure opens up the temptations connected with drifting.*

A number of my clients achieve something big and they complain that they don't feel as happy as they thought they would. I assure them that this is a natural occurrence for a significant number of people. It helps to *give up the fantasy of how you think you would feel upon achieving a Big Dream* — and then become mindful. Enjoy the moments! Enjoy the moments of striving, achieving and then celebrating.

By the way, *Take Control of Your Stories*. One of my clients complained: "I achieved a big dream I've held for years. But I don't feel fulfilled. I just hopped onto my next goals. I haven't stopped to celebrate my success."

I asked a number of questions including: "What would be a way to celebrate your success?"

After getting the client to connect with such a possible celebration, I said, "Schedule that celebration. I want to hear you *drop this story of 'I don't have time to celebrate.'* It is *not* serving you. Now, we'll write a New, Better Story for you. People who burn out get stuck in a Terrible Story." I continued, "Instead, for you, you might get tired. Then you rest up. Then you *Keep Up*. It's about keeping a structure of challenge, activity, recovery—and even fun. You rotate these elements."

Get It Together about Staying Rich. **What can you do to keep structure in your life? Rotate challenge, activity, recovery—and even fun. How will you take the next steps for these four elements?**

_____

_____

_____

_____

_____

Book Two: Work Smarter

Work Smarter #1

Get Real or Get Hurt—Get the False Stuff Out of Your Way—and Then Succeed

"Tell me something you know to be true, Tom," my long-time friend Sara asked.

"You need a good combination of optimism AND realism to do well in life. That's why I refer to myself as an OptiRealist," I replied.

I decided to write a speech on this topic:

"Get Real or Get Hurt:

How You Can Get False Stuff Out of Your Way

and

Create the Abundance, Success and Happiness You Want"

Reading many books each year, I'm drawn to those authors who tell the unvarnished truth. Why? So I can Save Time, Save Efforts, Save Money and . . . protect myself in certain situations.

That's why the topic "Get Real or Get Hurt" arose in my thoughts.

About "False Stuff," we can lose time, money and tears when we get caught up in false ideas, false methods and even false friends.

"It ain't what you don't know that gets you into trouble. It's what you know for sure that just ain't so." – ascribed to Mark Twain

I know the power of optimism. Without optimism, we do not put in efforts.

For example, I know someone, Eric, who had the optimism and vision that earning a masters degree in illustration would help him in his career. It's working. Eric is one of my team members working on my graphic novels entitled *Jack AngelSword*.

Still, we need strategies and realism to endure and triumph over the setbacks in life.

A novice speaker asked me if one needed academic degrees to be a professional speaker. I replied that a speaker needs Authenticity, Evidence and Experience. (I noted this as "A double E"—referring to A.E.E.)

My work is built on experience NOT theory.

In this section, I'll share a portion of my "Get Real or Get Hurt" speech.

The structure I use is:
- Myth
- A Way You Can Get Hurt
- Get Real Principle

Myth #1: If you do the right things, you can rest in the idea that your friends will stay for a lifetime.
A Way One Gets Hurt:
You'll waste time and you'll lose personal energy in

trying to please people who really cannot support you and cannot understand you.

Get Real Principle:
Be different—be YOU.

I learned the hard way that doing my best and doing a lot of listening to some individuals is *not* valued by them. One friend (who drifted away) told me at the end of a phone conversation: "That was largely useless."

I replied, "I do *not* do useless things. I care about you. If you have an emergency, feel comfortable to call me. But I will not be calling you."

This decision to separate from this friend did not arrive lightly to me. I had made efforts over more than two decades to keep being a good friend and keep listening. The truth was: this person did *not* value my listening. It was time to let the person drift away.

So I came up with this paragraph:

Some friendships are novels.
Some friendships are short stories.
Some friendships are a sentence.
Put a period on that and get away!

[Okay. As you notice, I'm using the word "sentence" with both meanings.]

The Get Real Principle is "Be different—be YOU."

When you are genuine and you support your real self, then you simply feel better.

You avoid twisting yourself for other people's approval. You'll have real friendships. You'll be strong, and you'll be okay if some friendships turn out to be short stories. When you step into a new chapter of life, not all of your friends will want to go with you.

Still, if you treat yourself like a cherished friend, you'll enjoy more moments of happiness and even success.

Now it's your turn.

Do you have any friendships that are truly unhealthy for you? What truth do you need to face? Do you need to limit your exposure to some negative people (even certain relatives)?

* * * * * *

Myth #2: You can make good money at just about anything.

A Way You Can Get Hurt:

You can lose a lot of time doing projects that do not yield excellent results because the pattern is self-defeating.

Get Real Principle:

Have a Good Business Model.

A close friend (I'll call him "Frank" and I mentioned him at the beginning of this book) died under tough circumstances. In his sixties, Frank struggled to barely pay his rent each month. Why? His business model was garbage. By this I mean, he was working too hard for too little return. There was no way to get ahead.

Frank wrote press releases. I'd ask him, "Can you go back to your previous clients and see if they have more work for you?"

"No," Frank replied. He explained that he could write the best press release, but if something startling happened in the news, his press release could be ignored. Frank was leaving a trail of unhappy clients.

"Frank, you've been a journalist for so long." I began. "You know how to coach someone to do well with the press, TV interviews and more. How about building up that end of your business?"

Sadly, Frank just "didn't get around" to making the needed changes in his Business Model [his system for earning income and running his business.]

Frank struggled greatly until his last breath on earth.

I helped Frank—for example, transporting him to the hospital and staying with him for five hours. Still, his business model caused great damage to his life.

On the other hand, a good business model looks like this:

• *You can get repeat business.*

• *You're building assets.*

(For example, my team works on my franchises (the assets): *Jack AngelSword, Jenalee Storm, TimePulse* and *Crystal Pegasus*. If you're curious, see the *Crystal Pegasus* graphic novel on Amazon.com. Franchises are often built on intellectual property.)

• *You're expanding how you serve clients.*

(A mnemonic device is "REB"—related to Repeat Business, Expand, Build Assets.)

Here's an example of "REB." I had the idea for a particular speech title. In the same week, I set an engagement to speak on that topic at a conference. Then in 30 days, I had a book completed and up on Amazon—on that new topic.

* * * * * *

Above, I've shared a part of my speech "Get Real or Get Hurt." (In a sense, this speech continues the work of my book *Darkest Secrets of Persuasion and Seduction Masters: How to Protect Yourself and Turn the Power to Good*.) In this section and at my blog YourBodySoulandProsperity.com, I write about practical ways one can increase prosperity. It does not have to be a serious, dreadful journey. **I hold to the idea of having a light heart and enjoying some laughter each day.**

Still, it's valuable to face reality and strategically act for your benefit and others.

Yes, I am an OptiRealist.

As an Executive Coach, I do a lot to help my clients use the strength of optimism and the effectiveness of realism to make their dreams come true. I often function as coach, consultant and mentor. I save my clients lots of time, effort and tears. My clients then get to focus their personal energy to leap forward faster. One client said, "Tom Marcoux coached me to get more done in 10 days than other coaches in 2 years!" – Brad Carlson, CEO of MindStrong, LLC.

Find your way to balance optimism and realism for your journey.

How will you build assets—and get repeat business?

_____

_____

_____

_____

Work Smarter #2

You Don't Need Willpower; Just Use a System and Get in Motion

"I just need more willpower. Then I'll write my book everyday," my client, Anna, said. In a discussion, I introduced Anna to the *Power of Having a System*. Research at Stanford University and elsewhere demonstrates that as the day goes on willpower "wears out." Dr. Kelly McGonigal writes that willpower is like a muscle that suffers from fatigue as the day goes on. I take advantage of this and eat salad for breakfast. And that is my "System"!

Myth: It's okay to wait for "One Focus," passion and motivation.

A Way You Can Get Hurt:

You lose the precious minutes of your life. You fail to get vital experience as your explore possibilities.

Get Real Principle: Get in motion; set a game; and set a system. (You don't need willpower when you have a system.)

Get in motion; set a game; and set a system. I use a mnemonic device to remember this: "MSG" as in *motion, system, game.* [Yes, MSG also stands for a food additive. Still, *Motion, System, Game* is an additive that BUILDS your life.]

1. Motion

Some people view the individuals like Steve Jobs, Tony Robbins, Martha Stewart and others to be a "force of nature." You do *not* need to be a force of nature. *To make progress, we just need you to take one step after another.*

3. System

Your system can take into account when you have energy. One of my clients writes her next book during her lunch hour. She found out that she feels too tired to write upon returning home in the evening—after her regular job.

Author Steve Chandler reports that he got a client to get invoices done by simply setting a pattern. The client now sends out an invoice immediately after a client call. The client does not stop even for the restroom until the email with the invoice is sent. Willpower is *not* required.

2. Game

A number of people allow their lives to fall into a pattern in which they cannot win. It helps to make a strategic plan so you can "Make it a game you can win." Pick a goal that is a stretch. Still, observe reality. Pay attention to feedback.

How can you get in motion? How can you "make it a game you can win"? What kind of system can you set up?

Work Smarter #3

Use "Both Ends Power"

Does the idea of setting a quota and having to fulfill it bother you?

The idea is to use *a Quota AND a Daily Journal of Victories and Blessings.* Why? If you only focus on a quota sometimes you'll go to bed feeling bad because you missed hitting your quota. For example, if your quota is to make 10 marketing phone calls, but you only hit 8, then you might feel bad.

However, if you write down 8 phone calls completed in your *Daily Journal of Victories and Blessings,* you can celebrate what you DID accomplish. Write down the good parts of your day in just 1.5 minutes—just before you go to sleep.

I refer to Quota plus a Daily Journal of Victories and Blessings as "Both Ends Power." Picture a ruler with quota on the left side. Your Daily Journal is on the right side of the ruler. I picked a ruler because you are measuring your incremental progress. Your Daily Journal helps you pay attention to your positive action. In this way, for 1.5 minutes a day you are celebrating your Daily Progress.

This ties in with using your brain effectively. Research shows that it takes 10 seconds of focused attention on something positive so that detail goes into your long-term memory.

So you are solidifying your impression of your progress—in your own mind. This is vital!

Myth: It works to continually punish yourself.

A Way You Can Get Hurt: You can de-motivate yourself and stop taking positive action.

Get Real Principle: Have a quota AND a *Daily Journal of Victories and Blessings* to record your progress. Keep up your morale!

What would you like as part of your *Daily Journal of Victories and Blessings* to make it a welcome part of your day? Are you attracted to certain designs? [Some people like flowers. Others like a design related to a theme park or a favorite film.]

Work Smarter #4

Make Sure You Have Reserves

"I'm in the business of *transformation;* I'm NOT in the business of Band-Aids," I assured a new client. Part of having the energy for transformation is to become strategic in how you build up your reserves.

To become truly successful, you need something: Reserves.
— Tom Marcoux

Reserves of what?
- Sleep (You'll likely awaken early on some days.)
- Ideas (You'll likely be confronted with a surprising problem.)
- Support (You'll likely have a close friend retreat— due to illness or family complications—or something.)
- Energy (To get things done, you must have energy.)

- Savings (To jump on an opportunity, you need cash reserves. Cash reserves help in crises, too.)
- Ways to bring in more income (The marketplace fluctuates all the time. You may lose a particular mode of income. Think of the people who sold ice—and then refrigerators arrived in daily life.)

Myth: It's okay to be haphazard about having reserves of personal energy, support, sleep and methods to bring in more income.

A Way You Can Get Hurt:
You can get blindsided and *not* have the reserves to recover.

Get Real Principle:
Every week, take action to build up your reserves.

How can you take action this week to build up your reserves of sleep, more ways to increase your income, and support in your life?

_____

_____

_____

_____

_____

Work Smarter #5

Challenge Your Habitual Thinking

"What would bring you peace, Tom?" my own coach asked.

Good question.

I have a question for you: **Do you have anyone who challenges YOUR *habitual* ways of thinking?**

I have a number of people who care about me who do NOT think exactly as I do. They bring good ideas to my attention.

When working with interns and contractors, I often do NOT offer my opinion first. I ask for their opinions *before* I voice my first thoughts. This method helps me *avoid* influencing their comments before they voice them.

Recently, I saw a video of in which young women were running a 600 meters race. With only 200 meters to go, a leading runner fell and hit her face on the running track. Did she stay there on the floor? NO! She got up and amazed everyone—in particular the other runners—by not only catching up, but running so fast that she came in FIRST.

The video included these words: "How determined are you to win your race?"

As an Executive Coach, my job is to help my clients look beyond their fears and limited perceptions. You can create Sustainable Wealth when you consciously take action to challenge your habitual thinking.

At the beginning of some of my speeches, I use a demonstration of a vital different between "Know How" and "Do Now." I show a pen and I say, "Do you know a way to remove this pen cap?"

I emphasize: **"We know too much; we're doing too little."**

I then show that you can move the pen cap by asking another person to help you.

Myth: You can figure it out by yourself with your habitual thinking.

A Way You Can Get Hurt:

You can get stuck and miss new opportunities for success and happiness.

Get Real Principle:

Consciously plan for challenging your habitual thinking.

How can you get people you trust to challenge your habitual ways of thinking? (You might get a coach.)

_____

_____

_____

Work Smarter #6

Focus on "What Reality Do I Need to Face?"

(also known as "How You Can Avoid Disaster—and Take BETTER Action to Enjoy More Success")

When the ember rose up, it fell toward a small area behind a mini-bookcase in Sam's living room. Sam, a friend of mine, had simply blown out a scented candle that his wife had left burning. Still, he was surprised when a bit of the candle wick (the ember) flew up.

Sam's wife said, "The ember went out."

Still concerned, Sam quickly grabbed the fire extinguisher that they stored in another room.

He remained in the room (with the now extinguished candle) and repeatedly checked to see whether or not the little ember had found dust to ignite.

Fortunately, no errant spark nor fire was ignited.

This story inspired me to identify these elements. When I speak on the topic "Get Real or Get Hurt: Get False Stuff Out of Your Way and Succeed," I begin with a "myth."

Myth: You can get by when you only seek ways to be comfortable.

A Way You Can Get Hurt:

A small problem may *grow bigger* and smother the goodness in your life.

Get Real Principle:

Keep vigilant. Ask yourself, "What reality do I need to face?"

Have you or someone near you said, "I knew I should have done something about that a while ago"?

That "something" is an ember that can start a raging fire—given time and fuel.

Many problems just get bigger with the passage of time.

I was talking with my coach and I asked myself a question (since I'm an Executive Coach myself). My question was: "What reality do I need to face?"

At the time, I realized that I need two opposing methods to insure both my continued efforts AND to keep up my own morale.

For my own business, I needed to increase the number of marketing phone calls that I made in a day. Prior to this, I had shied away from holding myself to a "quota of calls."

Then I came up with a process that I call *"Both Ends Power."* [I mentioned this in a another section.]

Picture a ruler. On the left end is marked "Quota" and on the right end is marked "Daily Journal of Victories and Blessings."

During the day, you make efforts toward your quota—for example 10 marketing calls.

At the end of the day you write down your personal victory "completed 8 marketing phone calls." The idea is to look upon the 8 calls as a Victory to note in your *Daily Journal of Victories and Blessings.*

Yes—I realize that one did not hit the ideal of 10 calls. Still, it's helpful to celebrate the 8 phone calls completed.

We're talking about a psychological truth backed by research: only punishing oneself does NOT ensure consistent, positive behavior.

We need to measure our behavior AND we need to pay attention to the "little wins."

Now it's your turn.

What can you measure? That's part of "what reality do you need to face?"

How will you note your "little wins" or victories? Will you consider noting each victory in a *Daily Journal of Victories and Blessings?*

With clients and audiences, I emphasize this idea: "Better than zero." If you are in the process of changing your behavior and placing new things into your routine, make sure that *you pay attention to your incremental progress.*

Research reveals that it takes at least *10 seconds of paying attention for a positive detail to get into our long term memory.* I advise writing in a *Daily Journal of Victories and Blessings.*

That's a great way to end your day. And that's the second part of the two sides of "ruler"—when we use the process of *"Both Ends Power."*

The best to you.

How can you keep vigilant? Remember: ask yourself "What reality do I need to face?"

Tom Marcoux

Work Smarter #7

Express Things Concisely

Recently, one of my Facebook contacts asked fellow members of the National Speakers Association about who would be a good candidate for a speaking engagement. I replied with:

"Susan, thanks for this alert. I've written 3 books on "making and keeping goals/resolutions" including *Emotion-Motion Life Hack, Nothing Can Stop You This Year!* and *Power Time Management* I walk the talk as a CEO, leading teams in 3 countries. I get results: "Tom Marcoux coached me to get more done in 10 days than other coaches in 2 years." – Brad Carlson, CEO I trained MBA students at Stanford University—15 year-member of National Speakers Association—winner of special award at EMMY AWARDS

https://www.youtube.com/watch?v=sjgoepLOz9c [link to 1.5 min. video]

My point in sharing the above comment is to show an example of expressing your qualifications concisely.

Express What's True for You Concisely

As I sat in the private luncheon of 203 people, former President Bill Clinton said, "If you cannot say in one minute why you want to be president, you don't know." His point was that you need to express yourself concisely and powerfully.

Two days ago, I responded to a post on author Ken Blanchard's Facebook page: "Congratulations, Ken [related to his new book]. And thanks again for your inspiration years ago. Since that time, I have been focused on my personal mission "I help people experience enthusiasm, love and wisdom to fulfill big dreams." My journeys have brought me to guest lecturing at Stanford University twice and speaking (15 years–member of National Speakers Association) and writing 35 books :) Thanks again, Ken"

Ken Blanchard taught me the power found in a concise mission statement, and that has served me for years.

At the moment, I'm working on a fantasy novel series

Yesterday, I was teaching my online class related to science fiction and fantasy to graduate students. In response to a question, I shared some details about one of my franchises: "It's a series of YA novels titled *Jenalee Storm.* She is a 17 year old in her first year of college. I focus on what "big thing" she needs to learn. This "big thing" will shake her up, cause some pain, and help her grow to a whole new level of personal strength and maturity."

I kept my post brief. People prefer brief.

Myth: People prefer to hear many details and the precise truth.

A Way You Can Get Hurt: You lose people; they tune out.

Get Real Principle: Create connection first, preplan what you will say to be brief and powerful.

What are you saying in a long-winded way? Fix it.

Work Smarter#8

Keep Team Members Engaged—Set up "Small Wins"

My team had been working for months on a graphic novel for children titled *Crystal Pegasus.* I had four colorists and a character illustrator and backgrounds illustrator.

How did I keep them motivated? I placed the pages at various stages of completion on a private blog. The team members could see what each was accomplishing. Having one's work on the blog was a "small win."

Myth: Everyone knows what incremental progress we're making.

A Way You Can Get Hurt: You lose good people because no one *feels good* about what's getting accomplished.

Get Real Principle: Set up "small wins." Make sure people can see quantifiable and incremental progress.

Recently, I shared with a friend some ideas about setting

up small wins for *yourself.*

My Facebook chat comment included:

"... Anyway, the idea about you doing some smaller versions of your projects in a short story collection was just an idea that came up in my mind during our conversation ... because you mentioned such "long haul" projects as graphic novels and you off-and-on text novel.

Smaller versions give you

- a "toe hold" in the marketplace
- a demonstration of a "paper trail" (you copyright an early version)
- a way to show family members (and others) that you're making progress
- a credit for your professional biography [I've taught such material in Designing Careers classes at Academy of Art University.]

What small wins can you set up for yourself and for team members?

_____

_____

_____

Work Smarter #9

Get the Right People Around You—and Listen

The Rich who lead teams successfully know one thing: You need to set up a climate in which people feel comfortable to offer creative ideas.

Years ago, a men's club was losing money because people were stealing bottles of shampoo. Someone even suggested setting up a camera system. To monitor shampoo?!

One custodian suggested, "Just leave the top off the shampoo bottle."

You want to have the right people around you and then listen to them.

I recall a great idea brought up by author Jim Collins:

You need to get the right people on the bus, the wrong people off the bus, and the right people in the right seats on that bus. [paraphrased]

Myth: People "know" that you value them and their input.

A Way You Can Get Hurt: Team members leave companies when the leader shows no appreciation.

Get Real Principle: Be sure to make it easy for people to provide each other with valuable feedback and even appreciation.

I belong to a Facebook group of authors-speakers. I had the chance to demonstrate how I *listened* to one of my top artists:

Speakers-Friends: I've learned that when working on book covers and "flyers" for our speeches and logos for our branded speech topics—we need a process in which we push beyond first guesses. For example, I had what I thought was a great idea for the cover of my new book—but my associate art director said the exact thing to get my attention. "That's good art, Tom. But it won't sell books." My concern was that the stereotypical star-field would feel so cold. Anyway, she pushed me to this cover. I did get something nature-oriented into the cover.
http://amzn.to/22kM03c

The above also reveals a great use of **concise phrasing to get your leader's attention!** ("That's good art, Tom. But it won't sell books.") And I praised my art director for her guidance.

How can you be sure to express appreciation?

Work Smarter #10

How You CAN Get Unstuck and Unleash New Opportunities for Yourself

Have you ever offered a friend a new idea and the person shot it down quickly? Perhaps, you started with "Have you tried...?"

And your friend said, "No. I tried that" or "That won't work."

Here's something worse: You likely carry an inner critic/cynic that shoots down ideas that could uplift your life.

How can we deal with such an inner critic who strangles possibilities and even prevents you from thinking in new empowering ways? As an Executive Coach, one of the major processes I offer a client is **to ask a well-formed question to open new possibilities for the person.**

Here are two questions that often lead to clients' enjoying *transformation*. [I say, "I'm in the business of transformation; I'm not in the business of Band-Aids."]

- What do you think is real that may not be true?
- How can you make it a game you can win?

1) What do you think is real that may not be true?

"Argue for your limitations, and sure enough they're yours."
– Richard Bach

How do you know something is real? Many of us base our perceptions on past experiences. I have even seen this pattern in so-called "experts." Many experts talk while they look at a "rearview mirror of history."

Think about it. People who create innovations are **not** stuck in "rearview-mirror" thinking! There was a time before iTunes and then **Steve Jobs with his vision moved through the resistance** of many in the music industry. Then, after Steve Jobs' persistence, we could have a song instantly available for just 99 cents.

How do you react when you hear a new idea?

Do you often react with "Oh, that won't work."

Consider using these questions:
- Is this true?
- How do I know this is true?
- Is it possible for something else to occur?
- Does someone on this planet have a different perception of this thing?

Years ago, I had a particular friend "Sam" who would shoot down any new idea. His whole approach was rigid.

I once asked, "Don't you think it's helpful to hear ideas from someone who doesn't think in your pattern of thinking?" Ultimately, Sam drifted away and out of my life. What a relief! Just before, he removed himself from my life, he said, "Where did my energy go? I had more energy in the '80s." In a conversation with him, I noted, "You were dedicated to something beyond yourself." I added, "Have you found someone new to serve?"

Now it's your turn. Do you have anyone in your circle who can offer you new ideas? Does anyone in your circle challenge you to think in new ways?

What do you read or watch on TV? Do you only look for agreement instead of looking to explore possibilities?

2) How can you make it a game you can win?

Several years ago, I was part of the team that set up the first bank with online banking. We did well. The management team said "Good work" and "Goodbye" to 30 team members. All of us were laid off.

I learned a number of things from that experience. One thing related to my role as an operations analyst who had a limited income. You can do your best, succeed with the project and be dropped by a corporation.

I prefer to build my own company because I make choices and learn—and build new skills and new possibilities.

My point is: Many of us have fallen into a pattern by default. Recently, I read part of a memoir of a CEO. He said that he had fallen into being a CEO.

Then, at one point, he allowed inspiration and intuition inform his transformation. It happened on a plane. He was reading an article on his way to an interview toward being the CEO of yet another company. While reading the article, he realized that he wanted new and different for his life. Just taking another position as a CEO would have become "same old, same old." Worse—he would feel dead inside.

Right there, on the plane, he made the decision to take his life into a whole new direction. He decided to become a coach to help others live their dreams and not by default. Yes—he sold the mansion and moved into an apartment with his wife (their children had already grown and moved out).

Here's my point: You can't "win the game" while you feel dead inside!

The late Dr. Wayne Dyer said, "You can NOT get enough of what you do not really want." He said that when he had difficulty with drinking alcohol, he could never drink enough to make himself really feel better. He did not want more alcohol. *He wanted a life of purpose, inner peace and joy.*

Now it's your turn. How are you living this chapter of your life? Are you devoting too much time and effort to what you do NOT really want?

How can you make some small changes? How can you "make it a game you can win?"

[Perhaps, you might feel better with this phrase: How can you change the pattern of your actions so you can enjoy each day?—the challenges and the fun parts of each day.]

Myth: It's okay to let any automatic cynicism shut down whether you consider new ideas or new possibilities.

A Way You Can Get Hurt: You can miss out on rising to a new level of success and happiness.

Get Real Principle: Consciously, double-check if how you're living is a source of positive challenge, accomplishment and even time to just breathe and enjoy happy moments. And if you feel unsettled, use that as fuel to explore new ideas, new possibilities and new actions.

I have another note about "What do you think is real that may not be true?" Today, I worked with a client on her speech about overcoming fear. I asked, "If fear should not be in control of your life, what is better to control your life?"

"My heart," she replied.

[That's how I work with someone on a speech. I help the person express something from the heart.] In conclusion, if fear is shutting down possibilities, ask yourself, "What could I make happen that is new—when I sidestep fear and move forward, listening to my heart?"

What do you think is real that may not be true?

Work Smarter #11

Open Your Awareness

"The law of floatation was not discovered by contemplating the sinking of things, but by contemplating the floating of things which floated naturally, and then intelligently asking why they did so." - Thomas Troward

You want more and better in your life—yes? Then focus on what you want and how to make improvements. I sat down with a prospective client, and we discussed my fee for a course of my serving as his Executive Coach. I said, "We're not going to focus on problem-solving. We're going to take this to the realm of **Solution-Creating.** We keep our dialogue going and we can find a *3ʳᵈ Alternative.* That will be something beyond our first comments." (That echoes the quote above about focusing on things which float naturally.)

We're talking now about opening your awareness.

Recently, I was invited to give an impromptu speech on the topic: "What would you tell your younger self and why?"

Here is what I said spontaneously:

"If I was meeting my younger self, I would have something to say that would turn around his whole paradigm of the way he looks at the world.

I would talk about how he can enjoy the journey and that the accomplishments are really *not* the most enjoyable parts of life.

I know that my past self was stuck in achieving, accomplishing, getting things done.

Later, I realized (and I learned this in particular by directing a feature film) that *the targets that I had were not the benefits that I got.*

I want to emphasize that: The targets that I had were not the benefits that I got from making the film.

The target of making the film was to make something that would serve lots of people. And it would serve to create a career which I thought that I wanted the most.

But I got an experience that taught me things that I could not imagine. It taught me how to deal with fear. It taught me how to deal with disappointment.

The experience taught me how to BE with what life gives you as opposed to trying to FORCE what you want upon life.

So I would suggest to my younger self that what I needed to learn and what I needed to experience was *beyond* my first imaginings.

And when you listen to effective people near you, your whole picture of the universe and what's possible expands. *That's* what the power of doing a project is.

Doing the project is not just picturing certain achievements, **it's about becoming a deeper human being and then serving others.**

I once had a friend who was really miserable.

I asked him, 'Have you found someone new to serve?' That's where the joy is and that's what I would tell my younger self."

* * * * * *

My above speech includes some insights that I only discovered by living them:

1. "The targets that I had were not the benefits that I got."

As I mentioned, I had certain targets connected to my writing, directing and producing my first feature film. The film did *not* jumpstart the film directing career I was aiming for—along the timetable I preferred. (I'm *still* in the entertainment field, and I'm having fun leading a team doing a trilogy of graphic novels titled *Jack AngelSword,* with plans for feature films. I'm also writing a YA novel.)

The benefits from doing many projects include, for me, my growth as a leader. My experiences as a CEO have made me uniquely qualified as an Executive Coach.

2. "The experience taught me how to BE with what life gives you as opposed to trying to FORCE what you want upon life."

Flexibility manifests an enjoyable, invigorating life. I've worked with clients who achieve something but find that they're not feeling as happy as they expected to. If we open our awareness, we discover that it's not about achievements, it about living in the present moment and enjoying the challenge, the fun, the surprises and the celebrating of what blessings do arrive.

3. "It's about becoming a deeper human being and then serving others."

"You want to set a goal that is big enough that in the process of achieving it you become someone worth becoming." – Jim Rohn

"We can have more than we've got because we can become more than we are." – Jim Rohn

When, I talking about serving others, I am NOT talking about being a martyr.

"You can help a thousand, but you can't carry three on your back." – Jim Rohn

Find ways to enjoy making a contribution to humankind.

Questions for Opening Your Awareness

A new client asked me a question about which of my books would I recommend to her at the present moment. I replied: "To find a relevant answer, it begins with questions for finding *your* answers:

1) What reality do you need to face?

2) What one thing if you truly handled it would create happiness in your life?

3) What one thing if you truly handled it would create the success you *really* want in your life?

4) What is in your way (obstacle) right now?

Myth: It's okay to focus only on the game of getting more toys, more money, more fun and more recognition.

A Way You Can Get Hurt: Focus on only selfish, surface goals leads to emptiness. Emptiness creates misery and self-sabotage.

Get Real Principle: Stay compassionate, stay open to Life's gifts and your opportunities to enjoy being loving and giving from your heart.

What do you need to make space for in your awareness and in your life?

Work Smarter #12

Your Springboard to Optimal Performance

I coach a sports psychologist who in turn coaches Olympic Gold Medalists. There is no Olympic athlete who avoids having a coach.

Top people in business have coaches. They know that they need to be at their best during *high impact moments*, which include closing a sale, getting new team members and successfully negotiating what you want.

Myth: Optimal Performance is possible without coaching and rehearsal.

A Way You Can Get Hurt: You can waste time, lose money and burn bridges if you go into *High Impact Moments* without coaching or rehearsal.

Get Real Principle: Get coaching and do some form of rehearsal *daily.*

Author Tony Robbins has talked about "The Science of Success and the Art of Fulfillment."

These two elements are central to much of the executive coaching I do.

"The worst days of those who enjoy what they do are better than the best days of those who don't." – Jim Rohn

What is it that you enjoy about your work? Become strategic in focusing on what only you can do. That's when you start to have a business!

Are you consistently getting coaching? Are you rehearsing for some High Impact Moment that's coming up on your calendar?

_____

_____

_____

_____

_____

_____

Work Smarter #13

The One Question that Leads to Real Success

In the recording studio, working on the end credits song for my first feature film, I made a huge mistake. I learned something that's benefited every subsequent project I've led. My learning has helped my clients I've supported as an Executive Coach and Spoken Word Strategist.

Here's what happened.

We worked on the song, and my good friend "Dave" sang during the chorus. He backed up the female lead singer. During the chorus I sang the low part in a three-part harmony. The chorus was sounding good! I was happy; I had written the song.

It's not until weeks later that I realized that the song was placed in a key that put the female lead singer's voice too low for the song. She didn't sound like a female during the verse sections of the song.

In few words, *I misled myself.* I made my friend Dave

sound good during the chorus sections. My focus was in the wrong place!

The lead singer must sound great!

I dropped the song from the feature film. What a waste of time and money.

It comes down to two questions:

1) What is Most Important here?

2) How can I get "fresh ears" (a fresh perspective)?

1) What's Most Important here?

On any project, we can get caught up in distractions. It's vital to keep asking, **"What's Most Important here?"**

As I illustrated above, I had been caught up in making my friend Dave sound good. And I dropped the ball on making the song work well.

This relates to the old phrase: "Win the battle and lose the war."

Be kind, for everyone you meet is fighting a hard battle. - Philo

Before I get stuck in regret about my error on the end credits song, it's time for me to "be kind" and to concentrate on the Most Important. As the director of the film, I simply replaced the song (with Dave on the chorus) with other songs from the middle of the feature film. So the film was not hurt.

The Most Important thing is that **I learned the lesson to keep the Most Important as my focus.**

I've learned to use a series of questions:

- What's Most Important here?
- Why is it important?
- How does this tie into what we value the most?
- What are the distractions?

- Is there something that I'm vulnerable to? (Some people are vulnerable to looking at a new idea as something that is "shiny." Any new idea may NOT be better. We recall that New Coke was not well-received. Ultimately, customers preferred Original Coca-Cola.)
- Do I need to get another perspective?
- Who do I trust to tell me the truth?
- How can listen to my true intuition?

2) How can I get "fresh ears" (a fresh perspective)?

How did I make the big mistake on the song? I did *not* have "fresh ears."

When working on a song, we put in long hours. We often suffer from "ear fatigue." I've heard team members lament, "I don't even know if it sounds good anymore."

It's important to take a break.

I remember when I was the lead singer of a band. The first time we went into the studio, I just didn't hit the notes correctly. I said, "That's it. I'll rehearse all week and we'll come back." That was a great decision.

I came back a better singer and with a fresh approach.

How do we know if something is working? Often we need to take a break to get a fresh perspective.

Recently, I was leading my team on an image (for a video) from my graphic novel *Jack AngelSword*. To get fresh perspectives, I had seven team members working on the one image.

An artist did not get the hero's facial expression correct. I brought in another artist to revise the face. None of my usual team members came up with a suitable body poise of the hero. I brought in another person to provide a fresh perspective.

My point is: We often need the input or effort of another person to raise the level of a project's quality.

Myth: Just barreling through and keeping to long hours is not a factor in making big mistakes.

A Way You Can Get Hurt:
You can lose lots of time and money when you have to throw out work that does not measure up and reach the point of excellence.

Get Real Principle:
Keep the Most Important as your primary focus. Take breaks and get a fresh perspective.

How can you put appropriate breaks into your workflow process? How can you get a fresh perspective?

_____

_____

_____

_____

_____

Work Smarter #14

Discover the Power of "Lead So I Follow, Speak So I Believe"

How often do you hear someone say something positive about a leader or a manager? Not often. Why? We have some subconscious expectations of what good leaders do. I coined this phrase: "Lead So I Follow, Speak So I Believe."

I have led teams since I was 9 years old, directing my first film. I've focused on being a good leader for decades. As a CEO, I currently lead teams in the United Kingdom, India and the USA. I've worked with mentors to develop my leadership skills. Further, as an Executive Coach and Spoken Word Strategist, I guide and support leaders to increase their impact and influence.

"Lead So I Follow, Speak So I Believe" is the experience that I want my team members to have. "I" stands for my team member.

Good leadership is NOT about the leader's ego. It's about making it possible to get things done and to have team members be clear about "the mission and the mighty." By this I mean, the leader shows how the team member can excel and "be mighty."

"Speak So I Believe" is about the team member believing that she CAN succeed. It's also about people believing that the project is worthwhile. No one ever got excited by a leader saying, "Come join us. We're doing something mediocre."

"Speak So I Believe" is about the team member believing that "I can trust this leader."

Nurture dialogue

"Whoever does the most talking has the most fun." – Ruth Reed

Good leadership is not focused on "slick talk." Many of us can see through that. It comes from empowering questions.

When you, as the leader, ask empowering questions, then the team member will have the fun of talking. More than that, you as the leader, will learn a lot about what is going on in your team and in the individual team members.

Use "Headlines" and "Taglines" ("Taglines get the dialogue going.")

An effective leader gives the headline like: "I'm now going to talk about three possible solutions to the XY situation."

Then, the leader shows that she or he is open to input by using a tagline like this: "After I discuss the three possible solutions, I'm going to open this up. I want to hear your ideas, thoughts and feelings."

How do you eliminate miscommunication and confusion?

When you express a headline, the listener understands your point up front.

When you use a tagline, the listener feels comfortable and primed to offer useful ideas for the discussion.

Start in a Positive Manner

As the leader, you set the tone. Do not let loudmouth team members start every meeting as a "complaining fest."

Instead, start a meeting with this question: "Who has an appreciation to mention about someone or something that's working?"

Myth: A leader can just wing it when he or she speaks to team members.

A Way You Can Get Hurt: You can lose the good will of your team members in a single moment.

Get Real Principle: Prepare your comments well. Work with a coach. Put in spaces so you can hear input from your team members.

How can you add "headlines" and "taglines" to your interactions with team members?

_____

_____

_____

Tom Marcoux

Book Three:
Drop What Does Not Work

Drop What Does Not Work #1

Don't Let Fear of Disappointment Limit Your Success

"I don't think I can take having my heart broken again," my friend Tabitha said. We had a substantial conversation. At a later point in our conversation, I shared, "Disappointment arrives in the chapters of our lives. It ultimately can't be ducked. The real choice is whether we chose to take appropriate risks. I came across an idea: Seek to be juiced, jazzed and inspired. That sounds good to me."

So pain and disappointment are coming. What can we do? Build up our reserves. Have you made sure to have enough support, exercise, sleep and nutrition in your life?

If you've moved to a new area and you don't have local

friends yet, you might need to hire a therapist or coach for the support you need.

Myth: Ducking disappointment will protect you.

A Way You Can Get Hurt: You *miss out* on great parts of life and live by fear instead of by courage.

Get Real Principle: Start with your heart. Focus on what you want in your heart and then approach the situation with "let's find out."

On a film set, I portrayed a character, David, who ducked out of the way of one punch, straight into the line of fire of a second assailant. BAM! the second opponent slammed his fist into David's face.

That's a metaphor for "ducking disappointment." I know a number of people who avoid taking risks and live a "quiet life." Instead of ensuring a comfortable life, they set themselves up for a *different form* of disappointment and trouble.

In trying to stay in their comfort zone, some people "blow something up" in their lives. If they became disgusted with their job, they do not leave in a cordial manner. No. They cause a disruption. Perhaps, they get sloppy in their work habits and fail to do a good job. In response, the manager fires the person.

Chasing meaning is better for your health than trying to avoid discomfort. – Dr. Kelly McGonigal

Tell yourself the truth. Is something becoming intolerable in your life? Is your work killing your soul? Do you have a friend who snipes at you and who drains your energy? Realize that taking some action and moving forward will feed your soul. How will you take action?

Drop What Does Not Work #2

Drop the Life-killing "Idle Rich Plan"

Best-selling author Randy Gage reported that his life started to become undone when he took time off and drifted without goals or purpose—after he had first become a millionaire. He noted that being idle was not a healthy situation for him.

Myth: Just relaxing is the life you want.

A Way You Can Get Hurt: You'll achieve a big income and then may fall into unhealthy habits that sabotage your success and happiness.

Get Real Principle: Rotate challenge, activity and rest. Structure is necessary for happiness and success.

Stephen, a multi-millionaire told me, "There's just so many fancy dinners you can eat. So many vacations you can take."

"You're looking for another mountain to climb," I replied. "You're right."

After multi-millionaire, author Stephen King suffered extreme injuries from a horrible accident in which a van slammed into his body, King's wife, Tabitha, knew what to do. She prepared a room so that *King could return to his writing*. Being idle was not restoring King's zest for life.

"Get busy living, or get busy dying." – Stephen King (through one of his characters)

"Don't wish it was easier, wish you were better. Don't wish for less problems, wish for more skills. Don't wish for less challenge, wish for more wisdom." – Jim Rohn

Here's how you can have more fun and increase your wisdom: Stay in the game. Pick new goals: ones that challenge you and excite you. Pick something that is bigger than yourself.

The secret is: Rotate challenge, activity and rest. Structure is necessary for happiness and success.

How can you rotate challenge, activity and rest?

_____

_____

_____

Drop What Does Not Work #3

Don't Wait to "Fix Something Broke Inside"

"I don't think I can get past this. I need some kind of shift inside before I can do better," my client Cindy said.

"I hear you," I said, before listening to some more details. Then I asked, "Would you like to feel better today? Are you willing to try something different?"

"Yes."

"Okay, this is advanced material. Life does NOT get perfect. We don't become completely free of old hurts. We can become much more skilled with living in the present moment. I remember an old phrase 'Prince Charming is not coming.' Later, I saw a feature film *Ever After*—starring Drew Barrymore— in which the princess Saved Herself.

How do you save yourself?"

"I don't know—study? Learn martial arts?" Cindy offered.

"Yes. In fact, I've helped women get scholarships to learn

a powerful form of self-defense. They've recovered their self-esteem after being attacked. I feel we need 'reading, writing, 'rithmatic and self-defense training," I said. To this day, I practice martial arts moves every day.

"Cindy, this is how you save yourself. Get in motion. Don't wait. Use a system."

Myth: You need to fix something broke inside to get results.

A Way You Can Get Hurt: You lose time to waiting for something to motivate you and "heal you"—so you stagnate in your waiting.

Get Real Principle: Set a System—"DDS" —"deadline, daily step."

One of my favorite quotes is: "In truth, I am a verb." – Steve Chandler

To me this means, I'm not a label, like one I had as a child: "shy boy."

No! If I act in courageous ways, I am a courageous person.

How about you? In what ways do you want to act? As a confident person?

One of my friends gave a speech in which she talked about her days struggling with depression and low self-esteem. At the end of the speech she said, **"I am FOR myself."**

I'll always remember that.

How do you act FOR yourself? **Treat yourself like you would a cherished friend**. You would provide good meals, a good place to sleep, and some fun moments for your friend..

Now, act in kind ways toward yourself.

Let's explore "Set a System—"DDS"—"deadline, daily step."

I just finished my 34th book. Did I feel like working on it this weekend? No. And that is an important part of getting past the myth "You need to fix something broke inside to get results."

"Inspiration usually comes during work rather than before it."
- Madeleine L'Engle

As I mentioned, "Deadline, Daily Step."
"Everyone needs deadlines. Even the beavers. They loaf around all summer, but when they are faced with the winter deadline, they work like fury. If we didn't have deadlines, we'd stagnate."
— Walt Disney

You can make progress by *Placing a System* into your life.

For example, I write every day. How? I keep a Progress Log of my writing. Additionally, I'll watch a few minutes of a favorite speaker expressing powerful ideas. I'll recharge, and BOOM! I'm back at the computer writing again.

How will you place a system into your life? What kind of deadlines will you use? You can start small. (For example, write 25 words each day.)

_____

_____

_____

_____

Tom Marcoux

Drop What Does Not Work #4

Don't Stick with Good; Step Up to Better

The Rich Don't Say: "I get bored easily." They don't say this because they don't want the Board of Directors to be afraid. A bored person might do something reckless. "New Coke" [the soft drink] comes to mind!

Here we are going to talk about how many people try to stay safe, and they get stuck in a rut.

The truth is "good enough" is NOT good enough in certain important situations. **If you have something creative inside that wants "a voice," be good to yourself and get started.**

At one point, I was too busy to write. Then I wrote this phrase: "Writers write or they're not writers, right?"

Silly?—yes. But I've been writing a lot ever since.

My concern for you relates to the idea of "taking the safe route." Often, the safe route turns out to be NOT safe. How? People start to become twisted inside. Why? **We were meant to grow, to explore, and have chapters in life that have new**

nuances. A new nuance could be taking your partner of 11 years and signing up for dance classes or Chinese cooking classes. How about both?! (or something else)

Myth: If you're good at something, you must stick with it.

A Way You Can Get Hurt:

You stick with something too long until it "blows apart" and someone gets hurt and trust is lost.

Get Real Principle:

Life is a series of chapters. A new chapter can start at any moment. You do better by leading your own transition.

What is going on in this chapter of your life? Are you near a breakdown? What do you REALLY want in your next chapter of life?

_____

_____

_____

_____

Drop What Does Not Work #5

When the Deep Lesson Raises You to a Higher Level

I learned something profound today. It was after I felt slammed down emotionally. Perhaps, you might find value in looking at *how some lessons arrive.*

It began about a week ago when I made a real error. Someone I'll call "George" came to me about a week before and said, "I could learn a lot from you. I'm making an XY project."

Suddenly, the excited educator in me (I do teach graduate students) went: "Oooh! I could save this person so much heartache, lost money and lost opportunities!" But I came on with too much excitement and energy. I admit it: I surprised myself by being "too much."

So I saw George today, and I apologized to him. He immediately told me a bunch of things that he feels that I do wrong. And I listened. Then, he said, "You've got nothing for me." And he accused me of not caring. *[What!?]*

Many of us who go into helping professions carry a deep hurt—that we hope to help others avoid. The truth is: **I care a lot and wish to help each person. Being kind is deeply important to me.**

In my childhood, I endured some bad things. I've written about how my father threw me, as a little boy, into walls. That was *not* love. [Other details, I'll leave *out* here.] My intuition picked up that George was deep into his own pain. **I've learned that there is no value in getting into a game of "my hurt is bigger and more important than yours."**

I felt that George had taken a rake and scraped out my heart. I have not felt this bad in one year and three months.

Then, later this day, I sat down with a dear friend, Rekha Raman. She told me about two ideas:

"Welcome and Release." – Rekha Raman

"When someone hurts me, a 'ghost' is created in my head."
– Rekha Raman

Welcome and Release

To me, it takes effort to welcome the lesson and even more effort to *release* the bad feelings and even judgments. Yes, I made an error, and I apologized for it. I do not want to fall into a hole of judgments against myself or George.

Still, the residue of the "rake scraping out my heart" could remain. I told George, "Don't care? You don't know me. You don't know what I've been through that has made me what I am. I seek to serve. I know we're not a match. I made a mistake. I was too excited. I wanted to be helpful to you."

In retrospect, I can imagine that George was not *with* me. George has his own pain.

I now have a choice. It is time for me to *release.* **What I want is to honor myself, honor George and honor the goodness of the Universe.**

I'll light a candle and say a prayer for George, me and the goodness of the universe.

I feel it's useful for me to *welcome the understanding* that I have certain hurt places in me that can be triggered. *That's the deep lesson for me to welcome.*

Still, I am glad that I did **NOT** react to George's accusations with any unkind actions.

I did excuse myself, and I stepped away from George.

"When someone hurts me, a 'ghost' is created in my head."

Because of certain social circles, I will see George again. I will give him space. He has told me off.

My intention is to focus on the people whom I can serve and with whom I can create a joyful energy.

If George and I talk again, I hope to *put aside* "any ghost in my head." (A number of authors write about forgiveness. I find the word *"free"* is made of letters in the word "forgiveness." I want to forgive myself and George.)

If George and I talk again — maybe I'll be in a better space; maybe George will be in a better space. Or maybe not.

I will enter each moment fresh.

And that, my friend, is something helpful.

Many blessings.

* * * * * *

So let's look at the above details and break this into the following parts:

Myth: Approaching each new person with your good intentions guarantees that you'll be treated fairly.

A Way You Can Get Hurt:

You lose a lot of time to feeling wronged. Further, you lose energy, and you simply feel bad.

Get Real Principle:

The Universe requires that you learn to shake off pain and move forward. You're required to forgive yourself, and often to forgive others. The alternative is to descend into bitterness and that causes a lot of pain and trouble.

How will you shake off insults and unfair accusations?

_____

_____

_____

_____

_____

_____

_____

Drop What Does Not Work #6

"Take Conscious Control of the Stories You Tell or They'll Strangle You"

As a boy, I grew up with violence causing harm to me. I'm not going to go into detail. Why? Because I'm NOT interested in reliving those details at this moment.

I will tell you that *I've gained empathy, resilience, strength, and compassion* from working with what I went through.

I also gained the ability to quickly assess situations and plan significant moves ahead. That ability truly helps my clients who seek me as their Executive Coach.

Here's my point. I do NOT speak in "victim stories." I'm *not* looking for sympathy. I'm looking to enter each moment fresh. I aim to be strong and support others to be strong.*

(* *I do acknowledge that therapy and medication can be quite helpful for certain individuals. I'm not a therapist. Some of my clients have me as their Executive Coach and they also see a therapist.*)

Take Conscious Control of the Stories You Tell or They'll Strangle You

I realize that the above statement may seem dramatic. But as a kid I experienced getting choked. You can't breathe. You can't think.

And a "victim story" restricts your energy and your thinking! It cuts you off from the life you really want to live!

What is the reality?

For years (several years ago), I told myself a story about a particular situation in which I thought I was only a victim. Then one particular, skillful therapist had me "re-experience" the incident – and FOR THE FIRST TIME, I saw that I took action. *I actually rescued myself* from more violence. I HAD A NEW STORY to tell myself.

Nothing had changed in the past. But now I had an Empowered Way to view my own behavior.

That opened a new, Empowered chapter of my life.

Let's go back to the question: What is reality? Was I always a person who rescued himself?

Let's pause a moment. Let's realize that Your Interpretation affects your personal energy and what you will actually do to stretch or *not* stretch yourself.

Do you have the energy to choose personal growth? Pay close attention to the stories you tell. Pick Empowering ones.

Myth: It doesn't matter much what you say. Words don't mean much.

A Way You Can Get Hurt: Your words can drain away your personal energy so you miss taking appropriate risks—and miss rising to higher levels of success and happiness.

Get Real Principle: Take Conscious Control of the Stories You Tell.

Which stories are best left out of your daily life?

Bonus:

Give from the Heart; Get Rich on the Way

"I want to get rich, but I'm afraid," my friend Wendy said.

"Of what?" I asked.

"It doesn't feel like a good thing, a ... noble thing to aim for," she said. We talked for a while, and then I shared with her an idea that had blossomed in my thoughts a while ago.

"Imagine this: 'Give from the Heart; Get Rich on the Way.'"

"What?"

"Start with your heart. What are you *called* to do? Who do you want to help? Then get rich as a part of the process," I said.

The 3 Elements of *Give from the Heart; Get Rich on the Way*

1. Pick something close to your heart so you devote yourself to becoming *good* at doing it.

"Writing isn't about making money, getting famous, getting dates, getting laid, or making friends. In the end, it's about enriching the lives of those who will read your work, and enriching your own life, as well. It's about getting up, getting well, and getting over. Getting happy, okay? Getting happy."- Stephen King.

Pick something that you love doing. You'll naturally dive deeply into the work—and you will get better! (Good coaching helps!)

2. Serve people on a big scale.

As of this writing, The Walt Disney Company earns $52.46 billion a year (2015). How? *They serve lots of people and they get a lot of repeat business.* And we're looking forward to more products and services. I own several Blu-ray disks that span Disney's subcategories: Pixar, Marvel, and Walt Disney Animation. I'm looking forward to attending more Disney Theme Parks in other parts of the world (for example).

If you're a speaker, song writer, singer—see how you might jump start your efforts with YouTube.com

3. Grow prosperous as you bring blessings to other people's lives.

Consider this question: *What can you do that's easy for you, hard for others and people will pay for?* It may be true that not many people find selling poetry to be lucrative. How about setting your poetry to music? People buy songs (for example). If you're doing something that's creative and meaningful to you, you're "winning," anyway.

"If you always do what interests you, at least one person is pleased." – *Katharine Hepburn*

I invite you to do what you need to do. Do a job that earns money to pay your rent AND explore other possibilities. This means so much to me that I wrote a book, *The Hidden Power of the AND-Universe.*

To truly make a positive impact, you need to give from an overflowing cup ... Enjoying more pleasure and abundance allows you to be the most generous. I know from personal experience that when you feel great contributing to others, growing your business is easy and fun!" – Vrinda Normand

Write down your first ideas in these categories:
1. Pick something close to your heart so you devote yourself to becoming Good at doing it.

2. Serve people on a big scale.

3. Grow prosperous as you bring blessings to other people's lives.

Second Bonus:
Guidance from Prosperous People:

10 Actionable Ideas
by Mark Sanborn, CSP, CPAE

1. Develop a growth plan with each person on your team.
2. Know thyself:
What time of day do you do your best work?
Make a list of the most important relationships in your life.
Compare your activity level to your accomplishment.
Identify your strengths, weaknesses, opportunities and threats.
What is your personal learning agenda?
3. Write a weekly appreciation note to someone on your team and/or a client.
4. Practice the "one a day" principle: find one person each day to do something extraordinary for.
5. Track the implementation of the "One a Day" principle: making it a point to do something extraordinary for a client or colleague.
6. Identify:
Key relationships to strengthen.
Key relationships to repair.
Key relationships to develop.
7. Think about and write down your three most important business metrics (how you keep score determines how you play the game).
8. Make a list of the 2-3 things that differentiate you from your competition. Are those differentiators valued by clients? Are they enough to give you a competitive

advantage?

9. Identify your value proposition: what value do you create for clients? How?

10. What are the three most important actions you'll take immediately to be a better leader?

Mark Sanborn is the president of Sanborn & Associates, Inc., an idea lab for leadership development. Leadershipgurus.net lists him as one of the top 30 leadership experts in the world. He has presented speeches and seminars in every state and 12 foreign countries. Mark is the author of eight books, including the bestseller *The Fred Factor: How Passion In Your Work and Life Can Turn the Ordinary Into the Extraordinary* which has sold more than 1.6 million copies internationally. His other books include *You Don't Need a Title to be a Leader: How Anyone, Anywhere Can Make a Positive Difference* and his latest book, *Fred 2.0: New Ideas on How to Keep Delivering Extraordinary Results Do.* Mark is a past president of the National Speakers Association and winner of The Cavett. Mark was awarded The Ambassador of Free Enterprise Award by Sales & Marketing Executives International. www.marksanborn.com

* * * * * *

Why Clients Aren't Paying You What You're Worth
by Jeanna Gabellini

Darn near everyone gripes about money. I do it, too. We each have triggers about making, spending and saving money. But the one I hear the most about is not getting paid enough. Either you have an abundance of clients but they don't pay you for the real value you give or you don't have enough clients and you're scared to charge what you deserve.

You might not even know what you deserve because you've been brainwashed to take what you can get even if you only end up making twenty bucks an hour in the end. Maybe a few people gave you feedback that they can't afford your services and products and now you're convinced that nobody will buy at your current prices.

There are more than a few reasons why your ideal customers don't pay you what you're worth and it's not because they can't afford you! Think about it. If they're your ideal customers, then they see the value in what problem you solve and joyfully say *"yes"* to whatever price you set.

If you're not charging enough you may need to:

1. Figure out the real cost of doing business. Include all overhead and time spent for every little aspect of delivering each product and service.

2. Nail down exactly what you need to take home each week.

3. Be more objective about the value your products and services give.

4. Lay out, on paper, the features and benefits of each product and service.

5. Charge from knowing what you want to grow into, not who you've been.

6. Consider yourself more of an expert in your field, even if you're a newbie. You bring something special to the table, no matter what stage of business growth you're in. When I was in coaches' training I was serving up breakthroughs for my "practice" clients long before I got my first paying client.

If your prices seem congruent with the value your products and services deliver, and not enough people are buying, you may need to:

1. Nail down your *ideal* customer and stop marketing and saying "yes" to those who don't fit that description.

2. Look at your beliefs about success, struggle, wealth and making a profit from what you love doing most.

3. Check in about what you offer. Do you love what you offer and the way you serve it up? How does your business support your desired lifestyle?

4. Clearly lay out the benefits and features of what you offer on all marketing materials. If you don't have bullet points on sales pages or brochures you probably aren't spelling it out clearly.

5. You're trying too hard to get clients. Pushing, needing, and worrying about getting money in the door comes from a place of lack and won't yield an abundance of anything (except heartache).

6. Tap into your Inner Business Expert and ask, "How can I align with more ideal customers? What should I shift? Is there an action that would serve me in this desire?"

There are more than enough people out there to pay you what you are worth. Before you go killing yourself to try a bunch of new strategies to figure out how to attract them, sit with the suggestions above and feel into which ones may be perfect for you to put into action. One baby step at a time will be sufficient.

When it comes to client attraction it always starts with your beliefs. More than likely, you need to expect more. Make bigger financial goals and play to win. Play with confidence. Abundant expectancy without expectation.

Jeanna Gabellini is a Master Business Coach who assists

conscious entrepreneurs to double (and even triple) their profits by leveraging attraction principles, proven strategies and fun. Grab her FREE audio on dialing in your biz at http://masterpeacecoaching.com/freecd

* * * * * *

(In line with the myth-busting in this book, here is guidance from Greg S. Reid.)

The Three Lies Motivational Speakers Tell
by Greg S. Reid

1) If you can dream it, you can do it.
Fact is, just because you dream of playing basketball like LaBron James doesn't mean that you can fly through the air and dunk the ball.

Know your limits.

Success Tip #1: Don't let OTHER people set those limits for you.

2) I know just how you feel.
Hogwash!

Only YOU know how you feel in any given situation, and feelings cannot be negotiated.

Explanation: Let's say you are sad. People may tell you every reason not to be that way, yet no matter how hard they try, you are simply sad.

Success Tip #2: It's OK to be comfortable within your own skin.

3) Natural Born (expert, leader, athlete, etc)
No baby was ever born where the Doctor said, "Oh my –

look, it's an accountant!"

Along life's journey we find what we are good at, and then do more of it.

This is how we build our competency, confidence and composure.

Success Tip #3: Work your strengths and hire your weakness.

Bestselling Author. Acclaimed Speaker. Filmmaker—
Greg S. Reid is a natural entrepreneur known for his giving spirit and a knack for translating complicated situations into simple, digestible concepts.

As an action-taking phenomenon, strategy turns into results fast and furious, and relationships are deep and rich in the space he orbits.

Published in over 45 books, 28 best sellers, five motion pictures, and featured in countless magazines, Greg will share that the most valuable lessons we learn, are also the easiest ones to apply.

He is an author of books in the *Think and Grow Rich Series*.
www.SecretKnock.co

* * * * * *

One line I learned from Legendary UCLA Basketball Coach John Wooden that changed my life!
By James Malinchak

I had the honor and privilege of having lunch with Legendary UCLA College Basketball Coach John Wooden (aka, "The Wizard of Westwood") in his Southern California home before he passed away.

Coach Wooden is arguably the greatest coach ever to coach in any sport, not just college basketball. What he achieved is truly amazing:

- 10 NCAA Basketball Championships
- 7 NCAA Basketball Championships in 7 Consecutive Years
- 21 Victories in the Final Four
- 38 straight victories in NCAA tournaments in 10 years
- Most consecutive victories in 3 years totaling 88 wins
- And more!

He was the college coach to basketball legends like Kareem Abdul-Jabbar and Bill Walton, as well as hundreds of others. He coached his athletes on what he called the Pyramid of Success. The pyramid is a collection of attributes that, not only an excellent team player must have to achieve success, but an individual must also have for personal success. These attributes include loyalty, friendship, enthusiasm, industriousness, initiative and several more.

Spending time with Coach Wooden in his home was one of the greatest experiences of my life. Not only did I learn much about the game of basketball, I learned even more about the game of life.

Coach Wooden taught me a philosophy that literally changed my life and has become a foundational principle for everything I do personally, professionally and financially. Here it is:

"It's what you learn after you think you know it all that counts!"

WOW! I meet so many people who say things like…"I've been doing this for 20 years so I don't need to continue learning"…or, "I'm already successful so I don't need to continue learning"…or, (fill-in the blank).

Top achievers not only make continuous learning a lifelong habit, they also understand that: *You don't go to school once in your life, you should be in school every day of your life!*

Coach Wooden is a legend in the athletic world, not just for all of his basketball successes, but also for his profound wisdom and life lessons!

Make a commitment to continue learning and investing in yourself on a consistent daily, weekly, monthly basis! Aristotle said, "We are what we repeatedly do. Excellence, then, is not an act, but a habit!"

I couldn't agree more!

James Malinchak is recognized as one of the most requested, in-demand business and motivational keynote speakers and marketing consultants in the world. He was featured on the Hit ABC TV Show, Secret Millionaire and was twice named "College Speaker of the Year" (APCA and Campus Activities Magazine). James has delivered over 2,000+ presentations for corporations, associations, business groups, colleges, universities and youth organizations worldwide. James can speak for groups ranging from 20-20,000. visit: www.Malinchak.com

As a consultant, James is the behind-the-scenes, go-to marketing advisor for many top speakers, authors, thought leaders, business professionals, celebrities, sports coaches, athletes and entrepreneurs and is recognized as "The World's #1 Big Money Speaker® Trainer and Coach" teaching anyone who wants to get highly-paid as a motivational or business speaker how to correctly package, market and sell their time, knowledge, experience, expertise,

message, personal story and how-to advice. visit:
www.BigMoneySpeaker.com and
www.CollegeSpeakingSuccess.com

* * * * * *

Interview with Michael Hsieh

Tom: What really moves your heart about your education project?

Michael: Seeing our country splinter between the haves and have-nots. As immigrants from Hong Kong, my family came to the US with nothing. My parents were driven to give me a good education so that I could succeed in America. Because they really supported me and pushed me to succeed academically, I was able to attend Harvard College and Harvard Business School and many doors opened because of that.

The opportunities for other people to do the same are becoming fewer and fewer. Because public schools have been decimated by a cutback in taxes, you can't get a quality education unless you have money or live in the right neighborhoods. I think teacher quality has also fallen. There is a myth that people achieve based on a meritocracy. I think so much of success is based on your environment and access to resources and knowledge.

I'm able to provide the same type of support to my own children but so many other kids do not have that. This lack of opportunities has created a tremendous wealth gap in our country. You see this now playing out in national politics and the presidential election.

I really wanted to do something about that. The opportunity presented itself when I was at a conference seven years ago. The founder of our school was speaking specifically about how our society is not a level playing field. Students of color in poor neighborhoods are set up to fail. The story we tell them is, "You failed because you're dumb or lazy." And that is not true. The founder of our school, Jeff Duncan-Andrade, is trying to reverse that narrative and provide resources to these families and children through a program called Step-to-College that had a tremendous record of success.

I thought, "Wow! What he is doing as an individual is incredibly powerful. We really need to broaden this and impact more students." He had it all thought out: the key is not to build a bunch of schools because all that does is create more haves and have-nots, the solution is to teach teachers how to educate these kids. Jeff incorporates colonialism, classism, and racism in his curriculum. These are the things that we don't like to think about or talk about, but they are very real in our society. Jeff builds pride and a sense of responsibility in his students so that they are motivated to get an education and return to help their own communities.

Jeff's vision was so clear and it had such great success— that I thought, "This is the mission that I'm truly passionate about." So I went up to him and I asked, "How can I help?" Being the teacher that he is, Jeff responded, "I don't know. You tell me how you can help."

Tom: Well done! That's *an educator. I can relate to it because I'm an educator.*

Michael: Yes!

Tom: This is a non-profit—?

Michael: It's a non-profit that has a chartered school at the center called Roses in Concrete. We're going to add other services like affordable housing, job training, medical services, healthy food.

Tom: Fantastic. I really appreciate that you're covering all these components because every element is crucial. Is there a time during your week, when you hear a story of something going right with the school, and it fills you up with energy—that you do better with your regular work?

Michael: I definitely get an emotional boost from working with the school. I'm not sure I can draw a direct linkage to my day job but the school clearly lifts up my spirit, outlook and sense of well-being. This spills over into everything I do, my relationships, everything.

The school feels so good that I just want to be there. When you're on campus, you can actually feel the energy and the enthusiasm. Every Wednesday morning I go to the school and do Drop Offs. As cars drop off the kids, I'm there opening doors and welcoming the children. That way I get to see the students and their parents. I can see the impact that the school is having on them. It's fantastic.

Tom: The reason I asked the question is that people will say that if they meditate and they reach some calm—that it will carry into the rest of their day. I was wondering if that is a thing that happens for you.

Michael: Yes.

Tom: If you were going to share advice or guidance to other successful people about doing non-profit work in their life, what would you say?

Michael: I think everyone is on their own journey. Just like I had to reach a point in my life when I met Jeff, I was drawn to him because I wanted to do something in education, and here came this opportunity—versus him coming to me and saying, "You should do this."

So I feel that the reward of non-profit work comes to someone who really wants to do something meaningful. When they are ready, the opportunity presents itself. So I talk to people about the school and if they are interested they will raise their hand and say, "I want to hear more. How can I be involved?" I then take Jeff's approach and say, "Great, come see the school and tell me how you would like to help." I think that is a much more inviting way of bringing someone in. When they're ready, they'll jump in with two feet.

Tom: Michael, thanks so much for sharing your insights with us.

Michael Hsieh is the President of Fung Capital USA, a venture capital firm in San Francisco. He has served on the boards of several non-profit organizations, including Chair of Center for Asian American Media, Head Royce School, University of San Francisco Center for the Pacific Rim, Wokai and Harvard Club of San Francisco. He is a founding board member of Roses in Concrete.
mhsieh@rosesinconcrete.org

* * * * * *

2 Quick Tips to Instantly Raise your Self Worth (and net worth)
by Morgana Rae

Here's today's Abundance and Prosperity tip. I received an email with this question:

"What's the quickest and most loving way to raise my self esteem and increase my sense of worthiness?"

I hear my colleagues talk a lot about how undercharging is a reflection of low self esteem, and how you have to increase your self worth to increase your net worth. I think

Suze Orman says something like that.

But nothing will lower your self esteem and self respect faster than undercharging!

I don't know about you, but I can't wait another forty years to resolve all my inner insecurities before I start making a living. So I'm going to give you a shortcut.

Wanna know my INSTANT, EASY strategy for a radical injection of self worth? Look OUTSIDE yourself for validation.

Surprised?

Here are some tips.

1) *CHANGE YOUR ENVIRONMENT.* (This is why I lead my retreat way out there in beautiful Bali.) Start eliminating the downers. This can be as small and simple as cleaning your desk, getting rid of ill-fitting clothes, letting go of "friends" who disrespect you.

20th century philosopher/physicist/genius **Buckminster Fuller** said that **"Environment is stronger than willpower."** You can try to think positive, raise your vibrations, and say your affirmations til you pass out; but your environment never rests. Those dirty dishes are working their black magic on your self worth even while you sleep.

It's really hard to feel abundant and prosperous with a dirty car.

Wanna feel better really fast? MAKE A LIST of ten things that rub you the wrong way. Nothing is too small. You have no idea how much energy the smallest things suck: If you live with a burnt out lightbulb long enough, dimness becomes "normal" to you, the best you can expect, and what you feel you deserve.

Make your list. Pick one thing. Fix it.

You will feel so much better, so fast, it'll give you a

surge of energy to tackle the next one. Work your way down the list.

Self respect is action driven.

2) *SEE YOURSELF AS YOUR MONEY SEES YOU.* If you have a romantic, loving relationship with your (personified) Money, your Money Honey will tell you how gorgeous, delicious, wonderful and desirable you are! Take his (or her) word for it. See yourself–and your worth–through the eyes of your beloved.

No one is more abundantly, scrumptiously confident than a person in love and loved. And it's fun.

A lot of coaches will tell you that all change comes from within. Uh, not really. Change comes from inside AND out. The world works its magic on us. **So why not stack the deck in your favor?**

Morgana Rae is an international #1 best selling author, pioneer in personal development, and regarded to be the world's leading Relationship with Money coach. Morgana's groundbreaking program for attracting wealth has featured her on ABC-TV, PBS, CNN, NPR, United Press International and The Wall Street Journal online. www.morganarae.com

* * * * * *

Interview with Ryan Peters

Tom: I know that your company is doing well. You're blossoming into other things. You have a partner who handles certain parts of your business. I'm wondering what is lighting you up now.

Ryan: In respect to my business, what's lighting me up ...

In the first five years, there was a lot of toil—and efforts—when there were not a lot of results and rewards. In Year 5 to Year 8, the company developed in a bit of a snowball effect. Like any relationship, as it develops and starts to prosper, we're really starting to see the benefits and results—That really lights me up. Not only to see a company that's making money, but to see a community and a culture that is bigger and stronger than any one of us individually. We do have such great individuals to make that community venture. That's part of it. And it's developing from a simple IT kind of a transactional product-driven company to more of a services-type of company that really looks at helping others in ways other than through products in the marketplace. We're getting creative in a bunch of different directions now. That's really fun!

Tom: You also shared with me, earlier, that you started with taking care of your employees with a nutrition center/restaurant. AND you've found a new way to build outwards from that.

Ryan: We started with a nutrition center/restaurant integrated in the company. It was based on some of my own experiences where I had to look at my own nutrition—getting older in my 30s. I'm finding that nutrition is more important than what it was like in my 20s. I couldn't survive on Big Macs, anymore. That was an evolution that I thought would be good to bring to people at a younger age, working in the company.

Also, we can help companies that we're working with to show them the benefits of bringing nutrition-related elements to their own employees—among other things.

Tom: That's what intrigues me. It's exciting. You can do something great, good for people AND do something great for prosperity, too.

Ryan: Yes, that's the goal for everyone.

Tom: Would you like to add something to what we've talked about?

Ryan: I always get asked what it takes to start a company. And it's like any relationship; it takes one step after another and some perseverance along the way. Eventually, it starts to work. I learned to recognize my own stubbornness and hardheadedness. I became able to step away from my own thought-process and to be able to say, "Look, maybe there's another way I should look at this." That goes back to the great individuals who make up the community in my company.

Tom: Thanks for sharing your insights, Ryan.

Ryan Peters is the Global Partner at Quadbridge Inc., a leading-edge, full-service IT Solution partner that specializes in hardware and software supply to medium and large enterprise clients in both the U.S. and Canada. Visit Quadbridge.com

* * * * * *

Consistency for Success
A lightly edited transcript of a video
by Randy Gage

Driving up the Florida turnpike to get to this Hilton Hotel [where this video is taped], a silver Chevy Silverado truck passes me. It slows down; I pass him. Two miles later, he's got to pass me and move over. It must have been eight times that this guy passed me in his silver pickup truck. And then I would pass him again.

The fascinating thing was I had cruise control on. So I never changed my speed. So he's just one these guys who has to hurry up and says, "I got to pass that guy!"

Instead, I had a relaxing drive, and I kept the cruise control on at the same speed. And eight times, I end up passing this guy because he's "stop and start, stop and start." And what a metaphor this is for a lot of people in life.

When I look at the businesses I'm in and the success that I've had with them—what's the thing that really worked for me? I have self-discipline. I'm willing to work hard. I apply myself. I have a vision. But more than anything else, I'm consistent.

I show up everyday, ready to play. If you want to be successful in sports, in the arts, in business, in any area of prosperity where you want to get to the high levels, you've got to be consistent.

You've got to show up all the time. You've got to pay your dues and do your homework. You've got to prepare yourself. And you've got to be in the game everyday.

We all can fall off the wagon now and then. I get that. But over all are you being consistent? For example, with money, I get a financial statement of my net worth from my accountant every month. Why? Because I want to know every single month that I've made some progress toward being wealthier. Even if it's only incremental. It doesn't matter. I need to see that financial statement every month. And that keeps me focused. It keeps me in the game everyday because I see that I'm always making progress.

So give yourself benchmarks to track. Give yourself some kind of accounting system. And then be consistent.

Thanks for watching.

Peace. Love you, guys and Live Rich.

Randy Gage is a thought-provoking critical thinker who will make you approach your business — and your life — in a whole new way. Randy is the author of ten books translated into 25 languages, including the New York Times bestseller, *Risky Is the New Safe* and *Mad Genius*. He has spoken to more than 2 million people across more than 50 countries, and is a member of the Speakers Hall of Fame. When he is not prowling the podium or locked in his lonely writer's garret, you'll probably find him playing 3rd base for a softball team somewhere. He was born in Madison, WI. www.RandyGage.com

A FINAL WORD AND SPRINGBOARD TO YOUR DREAMS

Congratulations on your efforts as your worked with the material in this book. To get even more value from this book, take the plans and insights that you created and place them in some form in your calendar or day planner. *Plan and take action.* Return to these pages again and again to reconnect with the material and take your life to higher levels.

The best to you,

Tom

Tom Marcoux

Executive Coach - Spoken Word Strategist

Special Offer Just for Readers of this Book:

Contact Tom Marcoux at tomsupercoach@gmail.com for special discounts on **coaching,** books, workshops and presentations. Just mention your experience with this book.

==> See an Excerpt from Tom Marcoux's book, *Darkest Secrets of Persuasion and Seduction Masters: How to Protect Yourself and Turn the Power to Good*—on the next page.

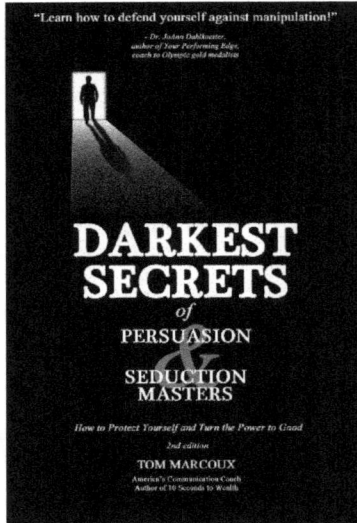

Excerpt from

Darkest Secrets of Persuasion and Seduction Masters: How to Protect Yourself and Turn the Power to Good
by Tom Marcoux, Executive Coach – Spoken Word Strategist
Copyright Tom Marcoux

. . . Now, I am in my 40's, with gray in my hair, and for 27 years I have been taking action to protect people.

And now is the time for me to protect you with the Countermeasures I reveal in this book.

Every human being needs to be able to break the trance that a Manipulator creates.

You need to make good decisions so you are safe and you keep growing—and you are not cut down and crippled.

This Darkest Secrets material is so intense that I first released it only with the counterbalance of my most energizing and uplifting books, *Nothing Can Stop You This Year!* and *10 Seconds to Wealth: Master the Moment Using Your Divine Gifts.*

An interviewer asked me: "Who can be the Manipulator?"

A co-worker, a boss, a salesperson, someone you're dating, and someone you think is a friend.

Now is the time—this very minute—for me to write this book to protect you.

I must speak the truth.

These Darkest Secrets of "persuasion masters" are …

Wait a minute! Let's say it plainly: These are the Darkest Secrets of masters of manipulation. Throughout this book, I will call these people what they are: Manipulators.

Dictionary.com defines "manipulate" as "To influence or manage shrewdly or deviously.… To tamper with or falsify for personal gain."

In this book, we will look on a manipulator as one who deviously influences someone with no concern about that person's well-being, and who causes harm to that person.

Here is the first Darkest Secret:

Darkest Secret #1:
Manipulators Make You Hurt
and Then Offer the Salve.

Manipulators would invite you to go out in the sun for hours and then sell you the salve to soothe your burns. The problem is that we don't notice that this is what they're doing.

For example, you're considering the purchase of a house. A Manipulator asks the question, "So, where would you put your TV?" This question is designed to put you into a trance.

Dictionary.com defines "trance" as "a half-conscious state, seemingly between sleeping and waking, in which ability to function voluntarily may be suspended." Let's condense this: in a trance you may not be able to function freely.

Here is the second Secret:

Darkest Secret #2:
Manipulators Put You into a Trance.

To protect yourself, you must learn to use
Countermeasures to Break the Trance.

All the Countermeasures (actions you can take to break
the trance) in this book will make you stronger and more
capable of protecting yourself.

Now, we'll view the third Secret:

Darkest Secret #3:
Manipulators Care Nothing for You and Human
Decency: They'll lie, cheat, and do whatever they need
to do so they win—but their charm masks all this.

Let's return to the example of a Manipulator selling you a
house. A Manipulator does not pause for an instant to see if
you can truly afford the new house. The Manipulator would
neglect to mention that you will not only have your
mortgage payment of $900. There will be additional costs:
home repairs, property tax, water, electricity, homeowner's
insurance, and more. The Manipulator only emphasizes
what he or she knows you want to hear: "Look! $900 is
better than the $1500 you're paying for rent, which is just
going down the toilet. And the $900 is an investment."

Let's go back to **Darkest Secret #1:**
Manipulators make you hurt and then offer the salve.

The Manipulator has you feeling good about the solution
(salve) and feeling bad about your current life situation.

How? A Manipulator will make you hurt through
questions such as:

• What bothers you about paying $1500 a month for rent?

(The Manipulator will use a derisive tone when he says the word *rent*.)

• What is *not* smart about paying rent on someone else's house instead of investing in your own house?

• How do you feel about your children walking in the neighborhood where you live now?

Do you see how these questions are designed to make you hurt enough so that you'll buy?

An interviewer asked me, "Tom, aren't these good arguments for purchasing a house?"

"What we're looking at is the *intention* of the influencer," I replied. "Let's look at our definition of a manipulator as one who deviously influences someone with no concern about that person's well-being, and who causes harm to that person. If the person truly cannot afford the house, he or she will be harmed by buying it. If the manipulator conceals the truth, the manipulator is doing harm. That's the important difference."

Some friends of mine are ethical and helpful real estate agents who truthfully reveal the whole situation and help the purchaser achieve her own goals.

In this book, we are talking about another type of person; that is, unethical Manipulators.

* * *

In any given moment, we need to remember the tactics Manipulators use. We will focus on the word D.A.R.K. so you can remember details easily and protect yourself from Manipulators.

D — Dangle something for nothing

A — Alert to scarcity

R — Reveal the Desperate Hot Button

K — Keep on pushing buttons

1. Dangle Something for Nothing

What do conmen and conwomen do to seize your attention? They make you think you're getting a "steal."

I recently saw a documentary in which a conman on a street in England showed a toy that looked like it was dancing. This fake product was actually dancing because of a hidden, invisible thread. The conman was dangling something for nothing. The Entranced Buyer thought he was getting something worth $20 for only $5. That was the trick. The Entranced Buyer felt that he was getting $15 extra of value for his $5. What the Buyer really got was something worth nothing. Similarly, I know someone who purchased a copy of a Disney movie from a street vendor in San Francisco. She brought the copy home and it was unwatchable—and the street vendor was never seen again.

An old phrase goes, "A conman cannot con someone who is not looking for something for nothing."

How to Protect Yourself from "Dangle Something for Nothing"

Stop! Get on your cell phone and talk through the "deal" with someone you know who thinks clearly. Go home. Think about it. Do some research on the Internet. Listen to your gut feelings. If the salesman or conman is too insistent, get away from that Manipulator. Get quiet. Have a cup of water. Cool down. Break the Trance!

Break the Trance and Identify the Crucial Detail

Earlier, I mentioned that a Manipulator puts you into a trance. An added problem is that we put ourselves into a trance. For example, as you read this, are you thinking about your right toe? Most likely not (unless you stubbed your toe recently). The point is that we only focus on a tiny percentage of what is going on in our life.

Around fifteen years ago, I caused myself trouble because I put myself into a trance. I discovered that under certain conditions, friendship can make you nearly deaf. Here's how: I was producing a song for a motion picture. A good friend was singing backup in the chorus. Because of our friendship, I wanted him to sound great. I completely missed the Crucial Detail. In this kind of situation, the Crucial Detail is that what truly counts is how the lead singer sounds! I made a song that I could not release. What a waste of time and money! I had put myself into a trance.

In any situation in which the Manipulator is "dangling something for nothing," we often fall into a trance and miss the Crucial Detail. The most important detail is *not* that we're saving money if we order before midnight tonight. What counts is whether the product creates a lasting, crucial benefit in our lives. And is the benefit of the product worth the cost? Some people even program themselves to make mistakes by saying, "I can't pass up a bargain." The bargain is *not* the Crucial Detail.

Secrets to Break the Trance

This is the process of B.R.E.A.K.S. It will help you remember the proven methods to break a trance.

B — Breathe

R — Relax

E — Envision

A — Act on aromas

K — Keep moving

S — Smile

Secret #1: Breathe

Remember Secret #1: Manipulators make you hurt and then offer the salve. The Manipulator wants to put you into a state of being that fills you with a sense of urgency and anxiety. Oh, no! I'm going to miss the sale!

Stop this highly vulnerable state. Take a deep breath. Do it now. Take a deep breath and let your belly "get fat" by filling it with air. As you breathe out, let your belly deflate. Breathe in through your nose and breathe out through your mouth. This is called belly-breathing. Repeat the actions of belly-breathing three times. Good. Now, do you feel different? Remember, when you are relaxed, you are strong.

Secret #2: Relax

You become stronger when you condition yourself to relax in the face of adversity. Researchers note that when an Olympic athlete is confronted with the most stressful moment in her life, she has prepared in advance. She has given herself ways to calm down. Two powerful methods are described in this section about B.R.E.A.K.S. One is breathing, and the other is envisioning.

A special part of relaxing is the effective use of your posture ...

End of Excerpt from

Darkest Secrets of Persuasion and Seduction Masters: How to Protect Yourself and Turn the Power to Good

Purchase your copy of this book (paperback or ebook) at Amazon.com or BarnesandNoble.com
See **Free Chapters** of Tom Marcoux's 35 books
at http://amzn.to/ZiCTRj

ABOUT THE AUTHOR

You want more and better, right? Imagine fulfilling your Big Dream.

Tom Marcoux can help you—in that he's coached thousands of people: CEOs, small business leaders, graduate students (at Stanford University) speakers, and authors.

Marcoux is known as an effective **Executive Coach** and **Spoken Word Strategist.**

(and Thought Leader—okay, writing 34 books helped with that!)

*** CEOs, Vice-Presidents, Other Executives, Small Business Leaders:*

You know that leading people and speaking at your best can be tough.

Marcoux solves problems while helping you amplify your own Charisma, Confidence and Control of Time.

Interested? Email Marcoux—tomsupercoach@gmail.com

Ask for a *Special Report:*

* 9 Deadly Mistakes to Avoid for Your Next Speech

*** Speakers, Experts - for a great TED Talk, Book, Audio Book, Speeches, YouTube Videos.*

Marcoux solve problems while helping you to make your

Concise, Compelling Message that gets people to trust you and get what you're offering (product, service, *an idea*).

Yes - the *San Francisco Examiner* designated Tom Marcoux as "The Personal Branding Instructor."

Marcoux is an expert on STORY. He won a Special Award at the EMMY AWARDS, and he directed a feature film that went to the CANNES FILM MARKET and earned international distribution.

(Marcoux helps you *be heard and be trusted*—a focus point of his 16th Anniversary edition book, *Connect: High Trust Communication for Your Success in Business and Life.*)

As a CEO, Marcoux leads teams in the United Kingdom, India and the USA. Marcoux guides clients & audiences (IBM, Sun Microsystems, etc.) in leadership, team-building, power time management and branding. See Tom's Popular BLOG: www.TomSuperCoach.com

Specialties: coach to CEOS * Executives * Small Business owners * Leaders * Speakers * Experts * Authors * Academics

One of his *Darkest Secrets* books rose to #1 on Amazon.com Hot New Releases in Business Life (and in Business Communication). A member of the National Speakers Association for over 14 years, he is a professional coach and guest expert on TV, radio, and print.

Marcoux addressed National Association of Broadcasters' Conference six years running. With a degree in psychology, Tom is a guest lecturer at **Stanford University**, DeAnza, & California State University, and teaches business communication, designing careers, public speaking, science fiction cinema/literature and comparative religion at Academy of Art University. He is engaged in book/film projects *Crystal Pegasus* (children's) and *Jack AngelSword* (thriller-fantasy). See Tom's well-received blogs

at www.BeHeardandBeTrusted.com

at www.YourBodySoulandProsperity.com

Consider engaging **Tom Marcoux as your Executive Coach.**

"As Tom's client for many years, I have benefited from his wisdom and strategic approach. Do your career and personal life a big favor and get his books and engage him as **your Executive Coach.**" – Dr. JoAnn Dahlkoetter, author of *Your Performing Edge* and Coach to CEOs and Olympic Gold Medalists

"Tom Marcoux coached me to get more done in 10 days than other coaches in 2 years." – Brad Carlson, CEO of MindStrong LLC

Tom Marcoux can help you with **speech writing** and **coaching for your best performance.**

As Tom says, *Make Your Speech a Pleasant Beach.*

Join Tom's Linkedin.com group: *Executive Public Speaking and Communication Power.*

At Google+: join the community "Create Your Best Life – Charisma & Confidence"

Get a **Free** report: "9 Deadly Mistakes to Avoid for Your Next Speech and 9 Surefire Methods" at

http://tomsupercoach.com/freereport9Mistakes4Speech.html

Tom Marcoux has trained CEOs, small business owners, and graduate students to speak with impact and gain audiences' tremendous approval and cooperation. *Learn how to present and get thunderous applause!*

"Tom, Thanks for your coaching and work with me on revising my speech at a major university. Working with you has been so enlightening for me. Through your gentle prodding and guidance I was able to write a speech that connects with the audience. I wish everyone could experience the transformation I have undergone. You have helped me discover the warm and compelling stories that now make my speech reach hearts and uplift minds. This was truly an empowering experience. I cannot thank you enough for your great assistance." — J.S.

"Tom Marcoux has been an NAB Conference favorite [speaker] for six years. And he is very energetic."
– John Marino, Vice President, National Association of Broadcasters, Washington, D.C.
"Using just one of Tom Marcoux's methods, I got more done in 2 weeks than in 6 months."
– Jaclyn Freitas, M.A.

Tom's Coaching features innovations:
- Dynamic Rehearsal
- Power Rehearsal for Crisis
- The Charisma Advantage that Saves You Time

Become a fan of Tom's graphic novels/feature films:
- Fantasy Thriller: *Jack AngelSword*
  type "JackAngelSword" at Facebook.com
- Science fiction: *TimePulse*
  www.facebook.com/timepulsegraphicnovel
- Children's Fantasy: *Crystal Pegasus*
  www.facebook.com/crystalpegasusandrose

See **Free Chapters** of Tom Marcoux's 35 books at http://amzn.to/ZiCTRj   Amazon.com

Your Notes:

_____

_____

_____

_____

Area for Your Sketches of Your Ideas: